365 activities
you and your toddler will love

365

activities
you and your toddler
will love

author
nancy wilson hall

consulting editors
dr. roni cohen leiderman & dr. wendy masi

illustrator
christine coirault

photographer
tosca radigonda

KEY PORTER  BOOKS

GYMBOReE PLaY & MUSiC

Produced by Weldon Owen Inc.,
814 Montgomery Street, San Francisco, California 94133,
in collaboration with the Gymboree Corporation, Inc.,
500 Howard Street, San Francisco, California 94105.

Gymboree Play & Music

Chief Executive Officer **Matthew McCauley**
Vice President, Gymboree Play & Music **Jill Johnston**
Merchandise Manager **Dawn Sagorski**
Senior Program Developer **Helene Silver Freda**

Weldon Owen Inc.

Chief Executive Officer **John Owen**
Chief Operating Officer & President **Terry Newell**
Chief Financial Officer **Christine E. Munson**
Vice President & Publisher **Roger Shaw**
Vice President, Creative Director **Gaye Allen**
Vice President, International Sales **Stuart Laurence**

Key Porter Books Limited

Six Adelaide Street East, Tenth Floor
Toronto, Ontario Canada M5C 1H6
www.keyporter.com

Library and Archives Canada Cataloguing in Publication

Leiderman, Roni
365 activities you and your toddler will love / Roni
Cohen Leiderman and Wendy Masi.

ISBN 1-55263-847-2

1 Toddler–Recreation. I. Masi, Wendy S. II. Title. III.
Title: Three hundred and sixty-five activities you and your
toddler will love.
HQ774.5.L43 2006   649'.50832   C2006-903460-5

THE CANADA COUNCIL | LE CONSEIL DES ARTS
FOR THE ARTS | DU CANADA
SINCE 1957 | DEPUIS 1957

ONTARIO ARTS COUNCIL
CONSEIL DES ARTS DE L'ONTARIO

a special note on safety

At Gymboree, we encourage parents to become active play partners with their children. As you enjoy these enriching activities with your toddler, please make safety your priority. While the risk of injury during any of these activities is low, please take every precaution to ensure that your child is safe at all times.

To reduce the risk of injury, please follow these guidelines: do not leave your child unattended, even for a brief moment, during any of the activities in this book; be particularly cautious when participating in the activities involving water because of the risk of drowning; ensure that your toddler does not place in his or her mouth any small objects (even those depicted in the photographs and illustrations), as some may pose a choking hazard and could be fatal if ingested; and make sure that writing and craft materials are nontoxic and have been approved for use by children under three years of age.

Throughout this book, we have suggested guidelines on the age appropriateness of each activity; however, it is up to you to assess the suitability of a particular activity for your child before attempting it. Ability, balance, and dexterity vary considerably from child to child, even among children of the same age.

While we have made every effort to ensure that the information is accurate and reliable, and that the activities are safe and workable when an adult is properly supervising, we disclaim all liability for any unintended, unforeseen, or improper application of the recommendations and suggestions featured in this book.

contents

12 months & up

1

18 months & up

91

24
months & up
181

30
months & up
273

Foreword

Welcome to the toddler years! Between the ages of one and three, children grow in amazing leaps and bounds. This is a magical time, as you and your little one laugh, talk, sing, discover, and find excitement in everyday moments. Playing with your child isn't just about fun and closeness, it's also one of the best ways to teach new skills, foster imagination, instill a desire to learn, and build self-esteem.

Many of the activities in Gymboree's *365 Activities You and Your Toddler Will Love* originated from Gymboree's popular Play & Music programs.

That means they've been tested on thousands of children to ensure that they produce smiles, giggles—and learning. We are proud to offer this book as a road map for the journey through your child's wonderful toddler years.

Let your imagination take flight. Expand on our ideas, follow your child's lead, and create your own adventures together. As you nourish your toddler's mind and enjoy special times together, you are enhancing your child's potential and building a lifetime of precious memories.

Dr. Roni Cohen Leiderman

Dr. Wendy Masi

12+
from twelve months & up

Your child begins her second year as a
great scientist, a fearless explorer, and an
increasingly independent person. She loves
achieving goals—even something as simple
as opening and closing boxes—for the sheer
joy of making things work. She's learning that
there's a world out there beyond your lap,
and she can't wait to experience everything
in it. But it's your support, and her love for the
people in her life, that give her the sense of
security she needs to confidently take her first
steps toward making the world her own.

1

mimic like monkeys

Little ones love to play "Monkey See, Monkey Do." Take turns mirroring each other's simple actions such as touching your nose and hiding your eyes, but keep the game from going on too long by using a code word to mark the end. How about "bananas"?

2

sing a counting song

"This Old Man" teaches counting, vocabulary, rhythm, and just plain silliness.

This old man, he played one,
He played knick knack on my thumb.
With a knick knack paddywhack, give a dog a bone,
This old man came rolling home.

In the next nine numbered verses, substitute the following phrases for "on my thumb":

Two...on my shoe
Three...on my knee
Four...on my door
Five...on my hive
Six...on my sticks
Seven...up to heaven
Eight...on my gate
Nine...on my spine
Ten...once again!

3

do a hat trick

A paper bag can become a hat in no time flat. Take a medium-sized paper grocery bag and help your child decorate it with nontoxic crayons; leave the top 6 inches (15 cm) of the bag undecorated. When you're done, roll the open end up the way you'd roll a pant cuff, and presto—a funny toddler-sized hat!

4

pour it on

Offer your child a shallow tray of dry cereal and a paper or plastic cup. Have him watch as you fill the cup with cereal then let him dump the cereal back into the tray. It's a physics lesson and a snack all in one.

5

track the train

This simple fingerplay gets 'em laughing every time.

The little train goes up the track.
walk your fingers up one of your child's arms
from hand to shoulder

It says, "Choo, choo!"
tug gently at your child's earlobe

And then goes back.
walk your fingers back down your child's arm and
make sure the train takes a trip up the other arm, too

6

make a beautiful noise

Let your toddler rock out in the kitchen with pots, pans, and metal measuring spoons to clink together; plastic containers to thump on the floor; and some sealed boxes of cereal and dried pasta to shake.

7

push and pull

Sit on the floor with your little one, face-to-face with legs spread and the soles of her feet touching the insides of your legs so that a diamond shape is formed. Join hands and do a gentle back-and-forth stretch. Lean back slowly (but not too far), pulling her toward you, then switch, letting her pull you as she leans backward. Finish by leaning in toward each other and sharing a kiss.

8

do a tickly fingerplay

Make this quiet or noisy, to suit your child's mood.

Round and round the garden
gently circle one of your fingers around
your child's belly button...

Goes the teddy bear.
...make more gentle circles

One step, two steps,
slowly walk your fingers up his chest

Tickle under there!
softly tickle your child under his chin

9

reach out for fun

Attach a couple of favorite toys to your child's car seat
with short lengths of ribbon or plastic activity links.
That way, they're at her fingertips for drive-time play.

10

"comfort me...
Get me back on track when
I'm cranky by pulling me into
your lap for a hug. Your support
helps me face the world—or at
least that jigsaw puzzle—again.**"**

11

create page-turners

Make turning the pages of board books easier for little fingers. Punch holes at the top of each page, thread them with yarn, then tie the yarn off and trim the excess. The yarn bumps separate pages so your child can easily find the delights hidden within.

12

inspire exploration

Explore a one-year-old's favorite concepts—open and shut, in and out—with supervised access to a variety of drawers, doors, and boxes. The better he gets at opening things, though, the more you'll need to lock up things that are dangerous or fragile. Consider devoting one drawer in the kitchen to your child, filling it with his toys and safe cookware to play with.

13

expand musical horizons

Add songs that aren't strictly kids' tunes to your child's
music library. Toddlers love lighthearted songs like
"Who Wears Short Shorts?" and "Octopus's Garden,"
and will respond to most types of music. Mix what you
love—jazz, country, rock, or pop—into the rotation of
little-kid classics, and involve your child by dancing with
her and clapping out rhythms. Soon she'll have her own
favorites, and one day you may hear one on the radio
and she'll gleefully yelp, "They're playing my song!"

14

march like a mallard

Chant and march to work off kiddie energy on rainy days.

Little Ducky Duddle went swimming in a puddle,
A puddle, a puddle quite small.
He said, "It doesn't matter
How much I splish and splatter
I'm only a ducky after all!"

15

go crackers about art

Invite your child to "finger paint" on graham crackers with yogurt or pudding. When he's done admiring it, he can eat his artwork.

16
pull my blanket

Seat plush animals in the middle of a blanket or throw rug and let your child pull them around the room. Then let her ride while you pull (gently and slowly).

17

blow some berries

When you combine a "raspberry" with a kid's belly, you've created one of the greatest sensory experiences a toddler can have. With your little one standing in front of you or lying on his back, pull up his shirt to bare his tummy, gently hold his hands, and blow a raspberry right against his belly. He'll giggle when you do it lightly, but you might want to experiment with using a bit more gusto, too. Chances are excellent that the noisier you get, the harder he'll laugh.

18

buzz a fingerplay

Here's one for your honey: sit facing
your child as you do this buzzy fingerplay.

Here is a beehive.
clasp your hands tightly together

Where are the bees?
hold your open hands out, palms up

Hidden away where nobody sees.
fold your arms across your chest

Soon they will come, flying out from the hive,
shade your eyes with your hand and peer out

One, two, three, four, five!
hold up your fists and open your fingers one by one

Buzzzzzzzzzzzzz! Buzzzz!
with both of your hands up, flutter your fingers

19

play with laundry

Toddlers love to help. When you're sorting clean
laundry, let your child pile socks or underwear into
a drawer or stack towels into a laundry basket. This
playful task gives him a chance to use his hands for
grasping and sorting, and it will make him feel like
a useful member of the household team.

20

scope out the haircutters

Your toddler is more likely to take her first haircut in
stride if she tags along on your hairdresser visits now.
Make it a positive event—sit her in the tall chair and let
her admire her reflection in the big mirror.

21

practice yoga

Get out some yoga mats or beach towels, take off
your shoes, put on soothing instrumental music,
grab a yoga book or DVD, and start stretching
together. Keep it fun, so the focus is on play more
than exercise. Don't worry about perfect technique
or holding poses for more than a few seconds.
Your child may enjoy yoga poses that mimic
animals, such as Downward-Facing Dog, Cobra,
or Cat. Finish with the Happy Baby pose—the
two of you can take turns *being* the baby!

22

drum some cereal

Have your child provide background "music" when you're hanging out together in the kitchen. Put some cereal in a large plastic sealable container, close it up, and let him shake away. For variety, give him wooden spoons to bang together or drum on the cereal shaker.

23

fly like a plane

Lie on your back and draw your knees toward your chest so your shins are parallel to the ground. Lift your little one up and lay her on her stomach atop your legs, hold her hands, and gently fly her like an airplane. While making sure she feels secure, offer her a peaceful glide or a rollicking, dipping flying adventure.

24

"look what I did... And I'm so proud! I love your praise, but sometimes my mastery of the world can be its own reward.**"**

25

share the social niceties

Understanding the social codes that help us get along with others will make your toddler feel like he's part of the adult world. So teach him to say "please" and "thank you" from the beginning, perhaps by playing games of handing objects back and forth. And most important, remember to say these words to him, too!

26

drop some clothespins

Select a widemouthed container such as an empty oatmeal carton, and offer it to your child, along with some wooden clothespins (the old-fashioned kind without springs). She'll have a great time putting the clothespins in and taking them out. Before long, she'll be standing and dropping in the pins from above, too.

27

march like ants

Get your toddler marching about the house as you sing and stomp this song together to the tune of "When Johnny Comes Marching Home Again."

The ants go marching one by one,
Hurrah! Hurrah!
The ants go marching one by one,
Hurrah! Hurrah!
The ants go marching one by one,
The little one stopped to beat the drum,
And they all go marching
Down to the ground,
To get out of the rain. Boom, boom, boom.
and continue, increasing the number and replacing "beat the drum" with

two...tie his shoe, three...climb a tree,
four...shut the door, five...take a dive, six...pick up
sticks, seven...pray to heaven, eight...shut the gate,
nine...jump out of line, ten...shout "THE END!"

28

bounce a knee ride

Try out this lively multicharacter knee ride, increasing your bouncing tempo for faster and faster riders.

This is the way the farmer rides—walk, walk, walk.
This is the way the children ride—trot, trot, trot.
This is the way the lady rides—a-canter, a-canter.
This is the way the knight rides—a-gallop, a-gallop.
And whoa!
dip your little rider between your knees

29

start stacking

Now's the time for your child to begin experimenting with stacking blocks. Start with small stacks and react to collapses with a light "Uh-oh!" to avoid frustration.

30

take the nut people swimming

Fill a dishpan with room-temperature water (outdoors, you can use a kiddie pool) and throw in a dozen walnuts in their shells. Add a plastic cup and a strainer with a handle for scooping up the walnuts. Give your child's budding imagination some room here—are those floating things the Walnut People? Fish in the sea? Boats? Caution: walnuts will stain some bathtubs and sinks, so rather than trying this in the bath, use a pan you won't mind discoloring. And always supervise water play and empty the dishpan or pool when you're done.

31

join the club

Waving good-bye, which most toddlers have learned
to do by this age, both demonstrates and allows your
child to practice important motor and social skills.
Not only is waving good-bye a pretty impressive feat
of coordination, it's also like joining humanity's big
social club by knowing the secret handshake.

32

get some kitchen help

Give your toddler simple tasks to do while you're
in the kitchen together. He may enjoy putting wooden
spoons in a plastic jar or oranges in a basket. Even
if he isn't actually helping, he'll be practicing
his eye-hand coordination and gaining a sense
of accomplishment as he completes his task.

33

learn about leaves

Collect leaves from your yard or a nearby park.
Look at them together, studying their shapes and
structures. In autumn, place dry leaves in a basket
or plastic container and let your child feel, smell,
and crunch them. In the spring, look for new leaves
just unfolding from their buds. Open up a bud to
show your child the "baby" leaf forming inside.

34

relax at mealtime

Want to keep mealtimes pleasant and avoid power struggles over food? Remember that a toddler can eat like a bird and still thrive. Don't make your child clean her plate—she's learning to listen to her body and stop eating when she's had enough, which is healthier than finishing food she doesn't want or need. It's perfectly normal for your child to go through some periods when she can't be bothered to consume more than a few bites, and some when she eats everything that isn't nailed down. You might prepare an alternative if you're serving something she doesn't like, but it definitely isn't necessary—or a good idea—for you to become a short-order cook to make sure she eats enough.

35

teach a merry melody

Chances are that by this age your child has a few favorite tunes that are staples in his repertoire. Spend a morning singing these favorites with him a few times then, while you hum the melodies, encourage him to sing the words. Or try leaving off the last few lyrics and have him finish the tune.

36

sleep under the stars

Place glow-in-the-dark star stickers on the ceiling above your toddler's bed. Make sure the lights have been on awhile before bedtime so the stars absorb enough light to give off a comforting glow in the dark.

37

crown me!

Make a crown for toddler royalty by cutting slits in the middle of a paper plate—first two that cross the center of the plate, then two more crossing these so that you create eight equally spaced points on the plate. Have your child color the plate with nontoxic markers or crayons, then bend the points so they stand up around the rim. Now stage a lavish at-home coronation.

38

cook up a pancake special

Make faces in pancakes by using berries or chocolate chips, and ask your child to name the nose, eyes, and mouth as you add them. Don't automatically offer sweet syrup—she may be perfectly happy without it.

39

sing a soggy song

This song is perfect for a rainy day.

It's raining, it's pouring,
The old man is snoring.
He went to bed and bumped his head
And couldn't get up in the morning.
Rain, rain, go away
Come again another day.
Little [your child's name] *wants to play!*

40

"enjoy my popularity...
But keep me from being
overwhelmed by friendly
strangers who want to play
with me before I'm ready."

41

get a sinking feeling

Fill a dishpan (or a kiddie pool, in good weather)
with water and, making sure you're always supervising,
bring out items for your child to experiment with.
Does a cork float? How about a potato? Try lots of
different toys and household objects, and sort them
according to what happens when they hit the water.

42

play "mirror, mirror"

Toddlers love mirrors. Ask your child,
"Who's that boy in the mirror?" Watch how he
reacts as you talk to him about his mirror image.
Ask, "Where's the boy's nose?" If he touches his
own nose instead of pointing to the mirror, he's
starting to identify himself as a unique person.

43

take piggy beyond the market

Just about every toddler relishes playing "This Little Piggy." To get more mileage out of the game, try drawing out the last line: "And this little piggy—that's right, this one right here, no, not that one, not that one, but this very little piggy right here on the end, oh yes, this little piggy cried 'Whee, whee, whee,' all the way home!"

44

start the day right

Routines give kids a soothing sense of continuity and predictability. A morning routine can gear your child up for the day ahead and, if it ends with one or both parents heading off to work, prepares her for the separation. So greet the day with a morning song, do stretches together, or go for a short walk to check the weather and retrieve the newspaper.

45

tuck baby in bed

Help your child make a snuggly bed for a doll or a plush animal using a shoe box and some of his smaller baby blankets. When it's nap time or bedtime, help him tuck in the "baby" before he gets tucked in himself.

46

find the toy

Spread a dish towel on a tray. Draw your toddler's
attention to a small, brightly colored toy. Play
with the toy together for a few minutes, then slowly
slip it under the towel while she's watching you.
Most one-year-olds will uncover the toy with a
flourish—she knows it is still there, even though
she can't see it. Once your child can do this
regularly, make the job of keeping an image of the
toy in her mind more challenging. Turn two plastic
cups upside down on the tray and slowly, within
her sight, hide the toy under one of the cups.
When she finds the toy consistently, she's well
on her way to understanding the concept of
object permanence (the idea that things and
people still exist even when they're out of sight).

47

hit the hardware store

What's better than a Saturday morning outing to the hardware store? The scent of freshly cut lumber, the dazzle of brilliantly colored paint samples, the feel of scratchy sandpaper. To adults and toddlers alike, a hardware store offers up dozens of sensory possibilities.

48

hang out in a hammock

On a sunny day—even a chilly one if you're armed with a cozy blanket—it's great to snuggle with your toddler in a hammock. For a little downtime, cuddle up and rock gently while you read a story together, talk, or just watch the tree branches swaying overhead.

49

make a shallow lake

Use a hose to make a puddle of water in a small tarp spread over grass. Add plastic animals, boats, and dolls, and watch your child as she rules (and wades around and sits in) her watery kingdom. Always supervise her carefully—never leave her to rule alone.

50

get to know a ladybug

Look for ladybugs in the garden, or make your own by drawing black spots on the back of red construction-paper circles and coloring in a black area for the head. If you do find some ladybugs, let your child hold one or two gently in his hand. Explain that they're good for gardens because they eat the little bugs that eat our plants. They don't bite us, though they may pinch lightly with their tiny jaws. Let your child sniff one. Yuck! Ladybugs don't smell good, but they're awfully good for our yards and gardens.

51

watch planes soar

Airplanes fascinate toddlers: after all, they're huge and they fly! Find a good viewing point (a park near an airport is ideal) and let your child study the planes as they pass overhead. Stretch her imagination by talking about where the planes might be going.

52

name body parts

Once your child can point to body parts like his ears, eyes, and legs, ask him to call out the names of those body parts as you touch them. Ask, "What's this?" then reinforce his reply by saying, "That's right. That's your nose." Then turn the tables and ask, "So where's my nose?"

53

"up and at 'em...
I love chances
to pull myself up.
And safe things,
like cushions,
to climb.**"**

54

nurture baby dolls

Children often enjoy learning to nurture babies.
Toddlers especially love to take care of someone who's
younger than they are, an activity that helps them
develop empathy. Tending to plush toys or dolls serves
much the same function—and they're fun to cuddle.

55

bag some toys

Hang a shoe bag—the kind designed to hang on
the back of a door—at your child's level. Invite her to
make a sorting game of putting away small plush toys
in the pockets. Line them up by type (for instance,
all the cats or bears), size, or color.

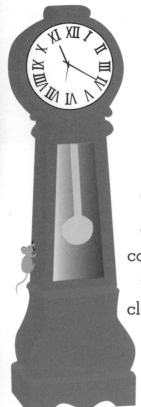

56

mouse around

This song is a fun way to expose your child to the concepts of numbers and counting. Make up extra verses to rhyme with the strike number, such as, "The clock struck two...the mouse kissed you."

Hickory dickory dock,
clap your hands three times

The mouse ran up the clock.
run your fingers up your child's left arm

The clock struck one,
clap once over your child's head

The mouse ran down,
run your fingers down your child's right arm

Hickory dickory dock!
clap your hands three times

57

build a kiddie library

Books on shelves can be tough to retrieve, so a big basket on the floor makes an excellent toddler library. As your child's storybooks multiply, rotate them so she doesn't get bored or overwhelmed (but don't put away all of her favorite books at once).

58

test while you play

Play games that help you track your toddler's visual development and hearing. Move toys back and forth and in and out of his field of vision, watching his eyes to see whether they follow the toy. To test hearing, lower your voice and whisper something—make sure he seems to hear and understand you. If your child's responses seem off to you, discuss it with your doctor.

59

be a massage therapist

To give your child a calming massage, undress
her down to her diaper and lay her on her tummy
on a soft towel on the floor. Warm a dab of baby
lotion between your hands, then stroke her back
from shoulders to hips. Although all toddlers are
different, many prefer a firm but gentle hand—not
at all rough, but not too tickly and light. Move
on to her arms and legs. Is she still awake?
Repeat the process on her front.

60

croon a lullaby

Not every song has to have a fingerplay or a bouncing
rhyme. A soft lullaby is perfect for times when your
child is snuggled close to you, almost asleep.

61

throw things

Don't let toddler experiments with gravity—otherwise known as throwing food from the highchair—get you down. You might want to discourage that particular activity by ignoring it, then rechannel his curiosity by taking him outside to observe how different things behave when he drops or tosses them. Cookies, rocks, feathers, and bubbles all move through the air a little differently—and every bit of that data will be filed away in your budding scientist's busy brain.

62

practice with cereal

Let your child practice her growing control of her
hands and fingers. Put a small handful of dry cereal
on a tray and demonstrate picking up the cereal
pieces, one by one. Drop a few into a bowl, pour
them out again, and let her have a try.

63

trot out a knee ride

Seat your toddler on your knees, facing you,
and hold his hands as you "trot" your knees
in time to this horsey rhyme:

Trot, little pony,
Trot to town.
Trot, little pony,
Don't fall dowwwnnn!

64

browse in a bookstore

Whether you pop in to check out the latest titles or come for storytime or a reading by a children's book author, bookstores offer lots of opportunities for fun and learning. Even if you don't manage to get out of there without some new storybooks, a bookstore visit is still inexpensive and valuable toddler entertainment.

65
sing dolly a lullaby

Nurture your child's tender side by singing to his doll.

Hush-a-bye, don't you cry,
Go to sleepy, little baby.
When you wake, you'll have cake,
And all the pretty little horses.
Blacks and bays, dapples and grays,
Coach and six white horses.
Hush-a-bye, don't you cry,
Go to sleepy, little baby.

66
do puzzles in pieces

The first time your child does a jigsaw puzzle, give her just one piece to fit. As her spatial sense improves, give her more pieces until she can do the whole puzzle.

67

get rolling

Outfit your child with a low cart that has a high handle—just right for him to grasp as he pushes it ahead of him. This kind of cart provides great stability for walking and, with a little imagination, almost unlimited play value. Today, it's a car; next week, a nest for a toy chicken and a plastic egg; next month, a garden cart for hauling sticks around the yard.

68

talk to the animals

Gather up some plush animals and arrange them in a circle around your child. Ask her to make each animal's special sound, then call on each one as if in a classroom: "Dog, you're next—a dog says...?"

69

have a rug toss

Throwing is easier than catching at first, and a small beanbag animal or a rolled-up scarf can be easier to handle than a ball. Bring out a few of them and a small rug or a bath mat. Ask your child to stand close to the rug and try throwing the animal or scarf onto it. Then move the rug a bit farther away to keep the task challenging and help him build his gross motor skills.

70

chill out

Your toddler needs a little "me" time now and again. So let her spend a few quiet minutes on a special blanket on the floor to give her a quick break from her busy day and let her practice amusing herself.

71

"let me get dirty...
Sometimes it's good to be
messy. But help me tidy
up afterward—clean feels
good, too!**"**

72

master advanced peekaboo

When your toddler is about a year old, she can understand that you'll still be there when you cover your face with your hands. She continues to love peekaboo, though, probably because she's old enough now to be in control and she may even initiate the game herself. Make it slightly more sophisticated by varying the way you play: peek around corners or over your newspaper.

73

carry some crayons

Time spent waiting for the pediatrician in the exam room might feel long and nerve-racking for your toddler. But you can turn it into playtime with a box of crayons. Why do you think that lovely long sheet of paper is there on the exam table?

74

build a nest

Too cold or rainy for your little one to play outside?
Gather up all the cushions you can find and, since
you're the big bird, build a nest for her in a quiet
corner. Add a few plush toys (especially if you have
toy birds!) and a little cup of birdseed (cereal or small
crackers). Try this in the middle of the afternoon and
be ready with a soft blanket so you can tuck in
your little bird for a nap in her nest.

75

read the signals

If your child turns his face away, pushes his hands out at you, or puts his fist up by his ear, it might mean, "Just give me a moment here, OK?" But if he's raising his arms to you, grinning, or bouncing excitedly, he's raring to go and telling you, "Bring it on!"

76

perform a bedtime ritual

Develop a nightly ritual to help your child wind down for sleep. It might be a story and a cuddle, a few minutes spent talking in hushed voices about the best events of the day, or maybe playing a CD with a favorite song that will become her good-night melody.

77

do a wishy-washy fingerplay

Wash the dishes,
wipe your hand in a circular motion one way...

Wipe the dishes,
...and back the other way

Ring the bell for tea.
mime ringing a bell

Three good kisses,
kiss your child on each of his cheeks and on his nose

Three good wishes,
tap gently three times on his forehead

I will give to thee.
point to yourself and then to your child

78

nip biting in the bud

Teething pain, the lack of an appropriate verbal way to express strong emotions, or even sheer exuberance can lead your toddler to (literally) sink his teeth into the world. Get to the bottom of his feelings, but make it clear that biting isn't an acceptable outlet for these emotions. If your child bites, gently take him to a quiet spot. When he's calmer, explain that biting just isn't OK—ever.

79

hammer it out

Hammering is terrific fun for your toddler, and it develops fine motor control and eye-hand coordination. Look for toy tool sets or pounding toys that she can use with your close supervision.

80

sing a song of fingers

"Where is Thumbkin, where is Thumbkin?"
raise your hands as if asking a question

"Here I am, here I am."
wiggle your left thumb, then wiggle your right thumb

"How are you today, sir?" "Very well, I thank you."
make your thumbs "bow" and "nod"

"Run away, run away."
hide both your hands behind your back, then
bring each finger out in turn and repeat with:

Where is pointer? Where is middle finger?
Where is ring finger? and Where is pinkie?

81

visit some animals

Take an excursion to a farm or a petting zoo, then ask
your toddler to name the animals he saw. Sing "Old
McDonald" and include the animals he met that day.

82

read together

Promote your child's love of reading by example. Have family reading times when everyone grabs a book and settles in. Your toddler can join a family member or look at a picture book on her own. Never leave home without a book to share with her in case you have to wait somewhere. In time, she'll come to see books and reading as one of life's great—and reliable—pleasures.

83

make a rainy-day sandbox

Set a plastic dishpan on a tray and empty a large box of oatmeal into it. Give your toddler cups and spoons for pouring and digging, plastic horses for grazing, or toy cars and trucks for tunneling through the oats.

84

follow the string trail

Kids love to explore, especially when there's
treasure at the end of the journey. Using a brightly
colored ball of yarn, wind a trail through your house.
Supervising carefully, help your child follow the trail
as it runs from his bedroom door, down the hall,
loops around the corner into the living room, then
winds in and out among the dining room chairs
until he comes to the yarn's end, hidden in a box or
bag that contains a small treat. If he gathers up the
yarn as he goes, the path will be easier to follow.

85

"encourage me...
It makes me feel great
when you let me know
about the new things
that I'm mastering."

86

choose some mood music

Pick different music to listen to according to your and
your toddler's activities and moods. Be sure, though,
that you enjoy times when the background noises are
turned off and your child can hear herself think and
listen to the natural sounds of her world. Give her the
gift of learning to appreciate silence.

87

paint footprints

Unroll large sheets of paper on a washable surface
(like the kitchen floor) and put a few colors of nontoxic
liquid paint out on paper plates. Let your toddler step
in the paint with bare feet and hold his hands while
he "paints" his footprints all over the paper. Then hang
his creation in his room, or use it for wrapping gifts.

88

try out new hairdos

Hang an unbreakable mirror on the wall behind
the faucet in the bathtub. To make washing more
fun, use the suds from tear-free shampoo to
sculpt hairdo shapes. Get creative with waves,
cone-shaped spirals—and maybe even horns or
a beard and mustache.

89

have a ball—or three

One ball is great, but a few of different sizes are
even better. For kids who have mastered standing,
kicking comes next. A soft rubber ball or beach ball
about 10 inches (25 cm) in diameter is perfect
for kicking. Smaller balls are good for dropping
and rolling, but be sure they're large enough
so that they don't present a choking hazard.

90

free the feet

Until your child is walking on her own out of doors, she doesn't need real shoes (nonslip socks or booties will keep her tootsies warm). When she goes barefoot in the grass, make sure the area is free of sharp stones, sticks, stinging insects, and litter. And check the sand at the beach—it can be hot enough to burn on a summer day. But as long as you're careful, you and your toddler can enjoy the barefooted pleasure of swishing through soft grass, padding along the water's edge at the beach, or squishing through mud after a rainstorm.

18+

from eighteen months & up

The 18-month marker is a real milestone for your toddler. His expanding vocabulary makes real conversations possible and often leads to a riotous exploration of humor. His increased mobility sometimes has the reverse effect of making him clingy, as if he wants to reassure you that he's not ready to go too far on his newly agile legs. Increasingly nimble fingers help him build block castles, throw balls, scribble art, pet the cat, and catch bugs. He wants to try and do everything, but he still likes you to be close by while he does.

91

have high tea

Your toddler's growing imagination and improving language skills can lead her to create delightfully elaborate tea parties. Let her use a toy teapot to help you pour "tea" into the cups of her "guests," and serve cookies or fruit. This isn't only pretend play—it's also great practice for future social occasions.

92

mind strangers

Your child will pick up on your behavior and level of comfort with strangers, so teach by example. Keep him close by when you're out and about so he can follow your lead about the people who make you feel comfortable and the ones that don't.

93

pack a travel tote

Stock a small tote bag with crayons, paper, a plush toy, a sock puppet, a book, a juice box, and a resealable container of cereal for your toddler. This portable entertainment kit is great for long drives or tiresome lines. Make sure she knows it's her bag—one day she'll even carry it herself!

94

pause for a poem

Your toddler will love the dramatic tension if you both pause for a second after the number "four" when you recite this poem.

The clock stands still
stand up straight and tall

While the hands move around.
move your arms around like the hands on a clock

One o'clock, two o'clock, three o'clock, four—
clap your hands with each number

Round and round, now touch the floor!
turn around on the spot and touch the floor

Cuckoo!

95

hit the beach

A beach is 360 degrees of pure surround sound—and surround smells, sights, textures, and even tastes (saltwater—what a surprise!). Protect your child with frequent applications of sunscreen, a T-shirt, and a floppy hat, then let him explore. Pouring, digging, and piling sand; feeling the water on his feet while you hold his hand; waving at gulls—all are great ways to expand his sensory horizons.

96

issue a command

Now that your toddler knows more words and has a
better memory, following commands can become
a game. If processing one task is easy, challenge her
with more complex instructions, such as "Put the
book on the table and the teddy bear on the couch."

97

get physical when you read

Reading to your child is about more than the words
you speak or the pictures he sees on the page. Help
him with language skills now and reading skills
down the road by bouncing him gently to keep time
with the words, emphasizing the language's rhythm
by repeating words that sound good together, or
tapping out the syllables on your child's arm.

98

make an animal farm

When is a shoe box not a shoe box? When it's a barn! Cover a box with red construction paper, cut out double barn doors and windows, and set it on green construction paper. Add a silo made from an oatmeal box, plastic farm animals, and a sprinkling of shredded-wheat "hay" for a complete farm experience.

play in the sand

For sandbox or sand-table play, give your child a variety of cups, funnels, empty spice jars with shaker lids, and colanders. Add water and supervise carefully as you let her explore all of sand's tactile possibilities by pouring, shaking, and shaping her "sandscape."

100

whip up some jellies

It's a snack! It's a toy! It's jellies!

4 packets unflavored gelatin
2 cups cold fruit juice, such as apple or grape
2 cups hot fruit juice, heated until just boiling

18+

18 months & up

The parent part: Pour the cold juice into a large heatproof bowl. Sprinkle the gelatin over the cold juice and let stand for 1 minute. Add the hot juice and stir gently but thoroughly until the gelatin dissolves. Pour into an ungreased 9-by-13-inch (23-by-33-cm) cake pan and refrigerate until set.

The toddler or parent part: Use cookie cutters (simple shapes work best for small hands) to cut out the jellies. Or just use a knife (definitely a grown-up job!) to cut the whole sheet into squares.

The toddler part: Poke the jellies with your finger. Stack them up and watch them shimmy. Bounce them off your highchair tray. Oh, and eat them, too!

101

"today I colored...
Let me talk about my adventures at the end of each day. It helps me exercise my memory—and it also helps me to unwind.**"**

102

fill some big shoes

Challenge balance, encourage imitative play,
and have a laugh: let your toddler take a walk in
Mommy's or Daddy's shoes, literally.

103

lend an ear

Reinforce your child's growing awareness
of what his body is—and isn't!—with this song.

Do your ears hang low?
Do they wobble to and fro?
Can you tie 'em in a knot?
Can you tie 'em in a bow?
Can you throw 'em over your shoulder
Like a Continental soldier?
Do your ears...hang...low?

104

paint a "watercolor"

Let your toddler "paint" the outside of the house (or the deck, the sidewalk, or the fence) with a bucket of water and a big paintbrush. This is especially fun on a hot day—and she can cool off by painting herself, too—but always carefully supervise any water play.

105

get creative with cups

One of the best—and least expensive—toy purchases you'll ever make is a set of stacking plastic cups. Besides basic stacking, they're great for molding sand castles, washing a doll's hair, holding a "lake" for tiny boats to float in, tracing circles, learning about sizes...you name it. Just hand a set to your toddler and watch what he does with them.

106

spin a spidery tune

For variation, try singing this popular song when your toddler is in the bathtub and encourage him to pour water out of a cup each time the rain comes down.

The itsy bitsy spider climbed up the waterspout.
"walk" your fingers up in the air

Down came the rain
wiggle your fingers downward to make rain

And washed the spider out.
make a "wipe out" gesture

Out came the sun and dried up all the rain.
form a circle with your hands above your head

And the itsy bitsy spider climbed up the spout again!
"walk" your fingers up again

107

do the wash

Toddlers love to imitate what you do, enjoy cleaning up, and are thrilled with water play. Combine all three by letting your child set up a toy laundry to wash his doll blankets, toy monkey's shirt, and plush puppy's ribbon collar. Give him a pan of warm water with just a tiny bit of soap, and another pan of plain water for rinsing. (Make sure you stay close by to supervise.) Improvise a clothesline, let him lay the items on a towel to dry, or help him pop them into the dryer.

108

lessen life's stings

Help your child cope with life's inevitable discomforts. After she takes a tumble, get down on the same level by sitting beside her or holding her in your lap. Acknowledge her pain ("That looks like it hurt!"), but don't fuss too long or too hard over minor accidents. With a scrape or cut, minimize the sight of blood by using a dark-colored washcloth to gently clean the area. When she's getting an injection, have her blow out as hard as she can while she's getting the shot. With a more serious medical event such as a painful ear infection or a cut that requires stitches, be her advocate and ask a doctor for the best way to relieve her pain. Studies have shown that healing is faster when pain is well controlled.

109

let your bookworm "read"

With you toddler's increased mobility and "busyness,"
he may have trouble sitting still during storytime.
One solution is to hold him in your lap and ask him
to read to you. "What do you see here?" you can ask.
"That's right—a billy goat! What's the goat doing?
What do you think he'll do next?" Let him decide
when it's time to turn to a new page.

110

teach the bare necessities

Though your little one enjoys trying to dress herself, taking clothes off is often much more fun than putting them on at this stage. Naked's great in the right context—so help her feel comfortable—but also explain that clothes are expected in most places. Going bare in the backyard now and then can make up for having to keep her pants on at the park!

111

hide and peek

While your child watches, hide two small toys in the room, and ask him to find them. Slowly increase the number of objects to keep the game challenging, but stop while he's still having success and fun.

112

sort it out together

Get your child thinking about how things are grouped into categories by having her help you sort clean laundry. Have her find all the socks or all the shirts and place them in a basket for you to fold.

113

get a good feeling

Collect small pieces of cloth and paper of different textures: velvet, sandpaper, cellophane, burlap, silk, tissue. Sit with your child and feel them together, one by one. "This one is smooth, isn't it? Does the sandpaper feel smooth, too? What about the furry one? It feels soft, doesn't it?" This stimulates his sense of touch and increases his vocabulary.

114

cook up a menu

Make a restaurant menu for home, with pictures of a few favorite healthy foods cut from a magazine. Present it to your toddler with a flourish at mealtime, asking, "What will you have today, madam?" Being allowed to choose boosts her sense of independence, but the menu's limited options help avoid frustration.

115

play with food

Use a nontoxic marker to draw a trail of large dots on a piece of construction paper, and put out a bowl of oyster crackers. See if your child can place one cracker on each dot. As his fine motor control gets better, use smaller foods such as dry cereal pieces.

116

jingle bells

Securely stitch large bells to circles of waistband elastic that are big enough to slip onto your child's ankles and wrists. Join him in some dancing and clapping so they jingle and jangle. Make sure you are always around to supervise his play with these bells.

117

splash up a storm

Fill the kitchen sink with warm soapy water and throw in some plastic cups and bottles. While you're right beside her, let your child stand on a chair (with its back to the counter for greater stability) and play in the sink as long as you're willing to stand there (don't leave her unattended though, not even for a moment).

118

"give me those gadgets...
Let me turn on your phone,
or stomp on the magic mat
that opens the store door.
I love trying to figure out
what might happen next."

119

dabble with paint

Cut pieces of string into different lengths, up to about 10 inches (25 cm), and dab them in pools of nontoxic liquid paint poured out on paper plates. Help your toddler drag the paint-covered strings across white or colored paper to create abstract designs.

120

outfit your handyperson

Equip your child with authentic versions of grown-up tools and equipment. Real but miniature garden tools, safe yet functional toy hammers and screwdrivers, and small brooms will help kids assist around the house. And toddlers love to feel like they're making a contribution!

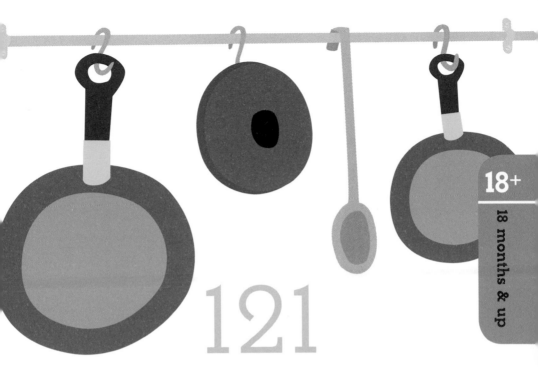

121

hail to the chef!

Your toddler will be delighted when you ask him to perform kitchen duty. He can put a clean towel away in a drawer, carry his unbreakable cup to the sink, or place rolls in a basket on the table. This is a great time to get him used to the idea that everyone can find a way to participate and lend a hand. He's also probably getting quite good at opening things, though, so be certain to keep all materials that might cause injury securely locked up or well out of reach.

122

blow some bubble art

Stir some nontoxic liquid paint into a little
bubble-blowing solution, and show your toddler
how to blow a storm of colored bubbles onto
a large piece of paper. Voilà—instant soap art!

123

shake a tambourine

Two paper plates and a handful of dry cereal
make a terrific tambourine. Give your child some
crayons to decorate the bottoms of the plates. Then,
with the cereal on one plate, use nontoxic glue to
join the plates together, making sure the decorated
sides face out. Secure by punching holes around the
edge and lacing the plates together using a long
ribbon. Now put on some music and get shakin'.

124

bond with some bugs

Lie facedown on the grass with your
toddler and put an embroidery hoop or a
loop of string on the ground in front
of you. How many different creatures can
you see inside this little universe? Are they
eating? Working? Just hanging out?
Those activities sound like the sort of
things you and your toddler enjoy!

125

offer a choice

Toddlers prize their increasing independence, but they also need structure. If your child wants to pick out her own clothes, narrow the choices: "Which will it be, the blue shirt or the white?" If she wants to pour milk on her cereal, give her some in a cup, not the whole carton. Let her make some decisions: "We need to go to the library and the post office. Which do you want to do first?"

126

stick on safety decals

Putting themed large stickers on a sliding glass door at your child's eye level serves a dual purpose: it will help him see the glass door, and studying and talking about the decals together will build his vocabulary.

127

hop on a bus

If you and your family go most places in the car, take a short trip with your toddler using a different mode of transportation. If you're city dwellers, ride a bus to a destination a few stops away or take the subway to the park. If you live outside the city, you might ride a commuter train into town or cross a river on a ferry. Supervise your child closely; hitting the road is fun but requires extra caution.

128

create new sounds

Collect three plastic film canisters. Fill one with buttons, one with bells, and one with marshmallows. Tape the tops securely, then ask your child to shake each one. Watch him enjoy the sounds he creates.

129

blow a kazoo

If your toddler can hum, she can also make music with a kazoo. She won't just broaden her musical experience, she'll also produce some great sound effects: silly voices get sillier, race cars become vroomier, and ducks are quackier with a kazoo.

130

share smooches

Kisses aren't just a sweet way to show your little one that you love him. Kissing takes coordination and shows social and physical development. When your toddler returns a kiss, it means things are coming together for him: lip control, trust, turn taking, and the ability to express his feelings.

131

sing royalty to sleep

If you have a son, you can reverse these lyrics
so you're the queen and he's the king.

Lavender's blue, dilly dilly,
Lavender's green.
When I am king, dilly dilly,
You'll be my queen.

132

make a bird snack

Encourage a love of animals by asking your
child to assist you when you go out to refill the
bird feeders and birdbath. To make a crunchy bird
snack, invite her to help you smear a pinecone
with peanut butter, then roll it in bird seed.

133

"let me cling...
Be patient with
me as I switch
between being
a brave explorer
and your little
shadow. **"**

134

make a library bag

Buy a plain sturdy canvas bag, and transform
it into your child's personal book bag. Use
nontoxic liquid paint to help her adorn it with
her handprints or with stamps made with apples
that have been cut in half and dipped in the
paint. Then use a fabric marker to add her name.

135

stack 'em high

Your child has probably graduated to stacking or
arranging about six to eight blocks by this stage.
Help build his architectural prowess—and his
understanding of size, shape, and balance—by
sitting down with him to build something a bit more
elaborate together, say, a castle or a skyscraper.

136

let your garden grow

Good garden help isn't so hard to find after all.
Young yard workers can pick up sticks, drop seeds
into holes in the soil, and water with a gentle
spray from a hose or a watering can.

137

create a land of cushions

Help your child build a place of her own out of all the sofa and chair cushions you can round up. Stand them on end for walls, stack them for towers or thrones, and strew them around the floor for magic stepping stones. If the walls come tumbling down? No harm done—just stand them up again or build something new and even more fanciful.

138

color in the snow

Tint water with dark food coloring and help your child use it in well-rinsed squirt bottles to "draw" on the snow or to "clothe" a snowman. She can also decorate snow figures with ice "jewels"— colored water that's been frozen in ice-cube trays.

139

greet another jack and jill

Is it a fingerplay—or a wingding?

Two little blackbirds sitting on a hill,
bounce your index fingers in front of you

One named Jack
wiggle one of your index fingers...

And one named Jill.
...and then your other index finger

Fly away, Jack.
turn one of your hands into a "wing" and flap
away, hiding your hand behind you

Fly away, Jill.
do the same with your other hand

Come back, Jack! Come back, Jill!
bring your "birds" back one at a time

140

explore a library's wonders

Your child can get a lot out of a trip to the library long before she's reading, so visit one regularly. You might ask about scheduled storytimes and activities for toddlers, or just go to take a look at the books. Most children's areas are noise-friendly and offer toys to play with and cozy reading spaces to curl up in. Some schedule short movies, picnics, or playgroups. The concept of borrowing a book and giving it back the next week is hard to grasp at first, but soon she'll be eager for "library day" so she can trade in last week's treasures for new ones.

141

draw different strokes

By the middle of his second year, your child probably
can hold a crayon (the chunky kind is easier for little
hands to grasp) and even make deliberate strokes on a
piece of paper. Demonstrate drawing a horizontal line,
and ask him to try following your example. Then do
the same with a vertical line. If he's enjoying imitating
your drawing, move on to a cross. Then let him cut
loose and scribble. (Bonus tip: if he decides to try out
his artistry on the walls, warming crayon marks with a
hair dryer makes them easier to wipe off.)

142

make a lantern

Have your child decorate a piece of paper with nontoxic markers. With her artwork on the outside, fold the paper in half crosswise, then cut 3-inch (7.5-cm) slits at regular intervals along the creased edge. Unfold and curl lengthwise into a loose tube. Fasten edges with nontoxic glue, stand the tube up, and admire her fine paper lantern.

143

avoid foul balls

Want a frustration-free ball game? Keep the ball from rolling off course by sitting across from your toddler with your legs open and his feet against the inside of your legs. Roll the ball back and forth inside the enclosed diamond shape that your legs form.

144

make a panda puppet

Fashion a panda puppet from a white lunch bag, black construction paper, and a red nontoxic marker. Open the bag but don't unfold the bottom. Put your hand inside with your fingertips in the still partly closed end of the bag, and you'll see where the face goes. Glue on two black paper shapes for eyes, two more for ears, another for the nose, a large black shape for the tummy, and two smaller ones for paws. Now draw in a mouth with the red marker. Make a few panda puppets and stage a puppet show with your child.

145

take a toy inventory

Make sure your child's toy box includes items that address a variety of developmental areas: blocks for fine motor skills; push toys for gross motor skills; materials for making or listening to music; lots of age-appropriate books; dolls and plush animals to encourage nurturing instincts; and playthings such as model cars, kitchen items, and dress-up clothes to promote imitative and imaginative play.

18+

18 months & up

146

welcome book choices

Encourage your child to look at books alone and to pick out ones you'll read together. You'll be surprised by how often his preferences change.

147

cook up some turtle pizzas

Take a softball-sized piece of store-bought or basic homemade bread dough and pull off about a quarter of that piece. Form the first, larger piece into a flat circle—the turtle's shell—about 4 to 6 inches (10 to 15 cm) across. Divide the smaller piece into six pieces. Use the small pieces to shape an oval turtle head, four legs, and a tail, and press them into their proper places on the dough. Spread marinara sauce on the turtle's shell, and have your child decorate it with shredded cheese, pepperoni slices, olives, or other toppings. Press two little olive bits into the turtle's head for eyes. Make a turtle pizza for everyone, letting family members choose their own toppings. Bake in a preheated 450°F (230°C) oven for 6 to 10 minutes, watching carefully to make sure your turtles don't burn.

148

"be my support...
I think I'm going
to be brave, but
then I get scared.
Thanks for not
laughing at me
or scolding me.
I'll be braver
next time!"

149

think inside the box

Toddlers this age love big boxes to play in, but don't expect complex imaginative play yet. Your child may not be ready to rocket to the moon in the box the television came in, but she'll relish the cozy space, the flaps to open and close, or maybe the chance to hide away for a nap with a blanket.

150

picture this

Put together a photo album of relatives and friends for your toddler. Look at it together and talk about the people you see: "Who's that? That's right, it's Aunt Kris—she's Molly's mommy." This type of album is especially good for kids with long-distance relatives.

151

recite a knee-bouncing rhyme

With your child on your lap and his hands in yours,

bounce this rhyme to teach the *feel* of language:

Intery, mintery, cattery corn,
Apple seed and apple thorn.
Wire, briar, limber lock,
Five geese in a flock.
Sit and sing by the spring,
O-U-T! And in again.
lower your child between your knees

152

"print out" a rainbow

Draw an outline of a rainbow on paper. Mix small
amounts of nontoxic liquid paint, and have your
child fill the rainbow with her colorful fingerprints.

153

walk and talk

As you're walking with your child through your neighborhood, tease his imagination and get him thinking about the people in his surroundings. Stop outside a house and talk with him about what might be going on inside: "I see a stroller. Do you think a baby lives there? And there's a leash on the porch—they must have a puppy!"

154

make a "quiet kit"

Place an activity basket near the phone to buy a few minutes of quiet when you have to make or take an important call. Include toys that aren't noisy, a small flashlight, and some sock puppets that only whisper.

155

dig some dinosaurs

Why do tiny people love enormous animals?
Maybe because in their budding imaginations
they're starting to see themselves as larger,
more powerful creatures. Your child may love
dinosaur toys, and, as he gets older—and
better at longer outings—he might enjoy
dinosaur events at museums, too.

156

do some target practice

Roll down the top edges of three paper grocery
bags to make a short, a medium, and a tall basket
for throwing practice. Give your child some
soft objects like sponges, and ask him to aim
at the shortest and closest basket first, then
move on to the taller targets farther away.

157

play some name games

Toward the middle of your child's second year, start
pointing out her name in print. Emphasize her first
initial and talk about other words that share the
same initial sound. "Dog starts the same way
your name does—listen: d-d-d-dog, D-D-D-Dana!"

158

save the bunny

This fingerplay appeals to kids' nurturing instincts.

In a cabin in the woods,
a small child by the window stood,
touch your fingers together to make a roof over your
head; use your index finger to draw the square window

Saw a rabbit hopping near, knocking at the door.
making a peace sign for the rabbit's ears,
"hop" your hand in front of you

"Help me, help me," the rabbit cried,
"I just need a place to hide."
throw your arms up twice in alarm

"Come little rabbit, come inside,
wave your hand toward you to beckon the rabbit

I'll take care of you."
cradle an imaginary rabbit in your arms

159

row that boat

Exercise your child's motor skills and balance
by having him "row" with a plush toy seated in his lap.

Row, row, row your boat
Gently down the stream.
Merrily, merrily, merrily, merrily,
Life is but a dream.

160

feel with feet

Broaden your toddler's sensory knowledge by giving
her a few large plastic tubs of squidgy, sandy, and
gooey substances like mud, sand, and jelly. Watch her
plunge in and explore the world anew—with her feet.

161

separate gently

The parenting books said your toddler would go through separation anxiety at nine months, and chances are she did. But she'll still have days when she clings, so respect her feelings and allow extra transition time when you need to leave.

162

play ring around the rosy

Gather a gang of kids and show them how to join hands in a circle and collapse at the appropriate time. Or grasp both your child's hands and dance around in a small circle just for two:

Ring around the rosy, pocket full of posies.
Ashes, ashes, we all fall DOWN!

163

"let's play hide and seek… I can explore what it feels like to be away from you as well as how great it feels to be found.**"**

164

pat that cake

This active version of "Patty Cake" is perfect
for your toddler's fine motor skill practice.

Patty cake, patty cake,
Baker's man,
Bake me a cake
As fast as you can.
clap your hands against his for the first few lines

Mix it up,
both of you mime stirring a big bowl of dough

And roll it out,
pretend to be rolling out the dough together

And mark it with a B,
use your index finger to trace the letter
in the air or on his tummy

And put it in the oven
both of you mime sliding the cake in the oven

For Baby and me!
gently poke his tummy, then your own

165

enjoy nature in the city

Can't make it to the wilderness this weekend?
A trip to a garden center is free entertainment,
though it may be hard to resist bringing home
some little green friends. Supervise closely as your
toddler wanders through a forest of plants. When
you're only a few feet tall, a leafy, misty greenhouse
becomes an Amazon rainforest, a tray of cactus is a
weird no-petting zoo, and the display of fountains
and birdbaths looks like a pint-sized lake district.

166

zip, snap, button!

At 18 months your toddler is developing the fine motor control and self-care skills to help dress himself. Find a book or doll that lets him practice with buttons, zippers, and other closures. Clothes that have roomy necks, big buttons, and zippers with large pull tabs help at this "I did it myself!" stage.

167

strum a tune

Make a nifty string instrument by wrapping several rubber bands lengthwise around a box with an open top or a hole in the top. A sturdy shoe box or a tissue box will work well. Supervise your child closely as she strums in case one of her "strings" comes loose.

168

check out the playground

A playground boasts more play equipment than you have room for in your yard, and often has a child-safe material underfoot to make falls less likely to cause injury. For a child this age attractions such as hiding places to look out of, low surfaces and inclines to climb over, and sandboxes to dig in, are great.

169

give kitty a thrill

Dim the lights and let your toddler provide a flashlight "mouse" for a cat to chase. This is a great way for a young child who might be a little nervous about touching a cat to interact with him. Besides, playing with a flashlight is always fun!

170

play favorites

There are times when only Mommy will do. Or only Daddy. Or only the babysitter. Don't be offended if your child plays favorites. She's getting to know the people in her life and learning to appreciate their different styles. It won't take her long to figure out that Grandpa swings her just right, or that Aunt Maria does the best monkey imitation.

171

jazz up a shirt

Keep the root end off a bunch of celery and help your child use it as a stamp to decorate a T-shirt. Dab the celery "stamp" in nontoxic paint and, with a sheet of cardboard inside the shirt to keep the design from bleeding through, stamp away. Once the shirt's dry, run it through a warm dryer for 20 minutes to make the design last longer.

172

make edible art

Finger paint with instant pudding. Strip your little one down to her diaper and give her some big sheets of paper and a plastic bowl of pudding so she can make some sweet artwork.

173

let those feelings out

Sometimes a day away from you may end with a
meltdown. Even if your toddler had a great time, he
may be tired and ready to release the strong feelings
that built up during the day. And who better to share
those feelings with than you, the person he feels safest
with? So if he needs to release a little steam, let him.

174

reassure your trooper

Your child's fears can be fickle: one day the neighbor's
dog and the giant model of the lobster are funny; the
next, they're downright creepy. Don't make a big deal
out of these fears. Just let your child know that she's
safe—and that you're there to look out for her.

175

do some milky magic

Pour a cup of milk into a shallow round bowl. Have
your child watch as you carefully—without
stirring—drop four drops of food coloring randomly
onto the surface of the milk. Then add a drop of
liquid dishwashing soap in the center of the bowl,
and voilà, it's tie-dyed (but not drinkable!) milk.

176

sing the abc's

Sometimes it's good to let learning creep up on your
little one. Sing the alphabet song as a knee-bouncing
rhyme, a lullaby, a jazz song, or even a pop jingle. In
two or three years when he's learning to read, he'll
realize that he already knows the alphabet.

177

be a little teapot

Mix up the usual actions to this ditty by having one of you act as the teapot and the other the tea cup.

I'm a little teapot,
Short and stout.
Here is my handle,
Here is my spout.
When I get all steamed up, then I shout,
"Tip me over and pour me out!"

178

tell it to the hand

Don a sock puppet and use it to ask your child questions about her life and daily activities. She may share some novel insights with her funny new friend.

179

do a spot check

Try out this activity to get a better sense of how your toddler sees himself and his world. Without him knowing what you're doing, sneak a dot of lipstick or face paint on his cheek or forehead, then put him in front of a mirror. Does he point at the spot on his image in the mirror or reach up to his own face? Sometime around the middle of your toddler's second year, he'll switch from pointing to the spot in the mirror to raising his hand to touch his forehead. Once this happens, you know your little one has begun to develop a sense that he's "me," his own person, separate from everyone else.

180

18+

18 months & up

"give me a play date...
People my size are
fascinating. Encourage
me to share and to treat
my friends the way that
I like to be treated."

24+

from twenty-four months & up

Your two-year-old's personality is blossoming a bit more every day. Children this age know their own minds and aren't shy about sharing opinions and intentions with you. However, you are still the lens through which your child sees the universe; your ideas and ways of interacting with the world help to shape hers. The big task for your toddler at this time is to learn about herself—what she likes and how she can participate in the world more fully.

181

wash the dog

If your dog is well behaved and compliant, letting your child help you wash her on a warm day can be a riot—and everyone gets a bath at once! Have on hand one dog, one toddler, the garden hose, dog shampoo, lots and lots of towels, and oh, yes—don't forget the camera.

182

march up and down

"The Grand Old Duke of York" is a great rhyme for older toddlers. You can bounce your child on your knee, let your fingers do the marching up and down his arms, or—even better for an upwardly mobile two-year-old—let him march up and down the nearest elevation, be it a cushion on the bedroom floor or a small hill in the park.

The grand old Duke of York,
He had ten thousand men.
He marched them up to the top of the hill,
And he marched them down again.

And when they were up, they were up,
And when they were down, they were down.
But when they were only halfway up,
They were neither up nor down.

183

work a wagon

While you're working in the yard, give your child
a series of small pickup and delivery jobs to
accomplish with her wagon. For instance, you might
say, "Pile up all the leaves you can in your wagon
and take them over to the trash can, please."

184

make a recording

When your child begins pretending to read—or
babbling as he follows the words—he has reached
a great milestone in pre-literacy. Don't slack off on
reading to him, though. Instead, add spice to the
activity by making a recording of yourself reading
his favorite books so he can practice following along
on his own when you're busy or away from home.

185

turn a negative into a positive

Your child's favorite word at this stage may be "no"—an outgrowth of her increasing sense of self and desire to shape her world. Let her assert the power of "no" by asking absurd questions like "Are we standing in the ocean?" so she can respond with a resounding "No!"

186

outfit your child for fantasy

Add four or five pieces of fabric, in a range of textures and colors, to your child's toy chest. They should be the right size to make a bullfighter's cloak, a butterfly's wings, a picnic cloth, or a plush animal's blanket. You'll be amazed at all the dress-up and pretend-play uses he'll find for these simple bits of fabric.

187

feed the birds

Open a restaurant for the birds. Put
up two or three bird feeders in your
yard, making sure at least one of them
is near your child's bedroom window.
Let her help you keep the feeders
filled with birdseed. Get a children's
book about birds from the library
and teach her the names of your
most frequent visitors.

24+

24 months & up

188

pamper your pets

It's not too early to involve your toddler in the care of family pets. A two-year-old can roll a ball or drag a piece of ribbon for the cat, or pour a cup of kibble into the dog's bowl. Children at this age also love to give treats, praise, and comfort to pets. Teach patience and gentleness, but keep your child safe by instructing him never to bother an animal that's eating or sleeping—and by supervising all close encounters of the furry kind. Don't overreact if a provoked cat scratches or a dog nips lightly—if you do, the child may become fearful. Say something like, "Ooh, Tux got scared when he felt his tail being pulled—let's pet him gently on the back next time and go put something on that scratch."

189

shake some maracas

Help your child make maracas by dropping dried beans, lentils, or unpopped popcorn into a small plastic water bottle. Glue or tape the lid in place securely and watch as your child plays to make sure the lid doesn't come loose, as small items can be dangerous if they find their way into small mouths.

190

seek out shapes

Play a game to hone your child's ability to recognize shapes. Start with an easy one on a picture-book page ("Can you find something shaped like a circle?") and graduate to finding circles, squares, and other shapes out in the real world. "How about that flower box? That's right, it's a rectangle. What about the moon?"

191

try a freeze

Teach your child about the transforming power of cold by helping her pour fruit juice from a lightweight pitcher into small paper cups. Then freeze the juice, adding wooden popsicle sticks once it's slushy. Waiting for these to freeze is hard, but worth it. It's also fun to let the cups harden outside on a very cold winter's day.

192

follow a pattern

Build on your child's growing understanding of patterns by getting ambitious with bead stringing. Using large wooden beads or spools, suggest an easy pattern like round-square-round-square. Or help him to put different colors in order—say, green-blue-green.

193

24+

24 months & up

" crack me up...
I laugh when the people I
love laugh, and also if you
do something crazy, like
offer a cookie to my elbow. **"**

194

solve a mystery

Hone your child's observation and logic skills by putting three plush animals in front of her and asking her to study them. Then have her close her eyes while you remove one. Ask, "OK—take a look now—who's missing?" Once she masters the game, make it more challenging by adding more animals.

195

make things larger than life

Give your toddler a plastic magnifier so he can see things he's never seen before. Looking at his own hand, a teddy bear's fur, or blades of grass will open up whole new tiny worlds to him. A small unbreakable magnifier of his own might even become one of your child's prized possessions.

196

run a toy hospital

Two-year-olds are very caring and often want to fix things that are broken. Encourage your child's nurturing side by asking him to help you take care of plush animals or dolls. Let him tuck them into shoe-box beds while they recover, then get them all up to celebrate their restored health with a snack.

197

get handy

Coat your child's hands with nontoxic liquid paint
and ask her to press them on a sheet of paper.
Handprints alone are great designs, but you can help
her get fancier by making tulips (fingers pointing
upward, with a brush-stroke green stem added
afterward); butterflies (two hands, wrist to wrist, with
the fingers pointing away from each other); or
a sunflower (several yellow-painted handprints,
fingers spread out, with an added brown center).

198

pet some rocks

Let your child paint smooth rocks with nontoxic paint.
He can decorate them with abstract designs or turn
them into creatures such as ladybugs, cats, or birds.

199

be a pea counter

This fingerplay sneaks in some counting practice:

Five fat peas in a pea pod pressed,
hold up one of your hands and make a fist

One grew, two grew, so did all the rest.
hold your thumb and fingers up, one by one

They grew and grew and did not stop
raise your hand in the air very slowly

Until one day the pod went POP!
clap your hands together loudly

200

make your child a star

Help build your toddler's sense of self by filming
her as she sings a song or tells a story. Play it
back for her so she can watch herself in action.

201

get bouncy

At around two years of age your child may start being able to bounce a ball and catch it, or to catch one that you gently bounce to him. Just bouncing the ball is feat enough for a toddler, so don't be too worried about where it goes. And remember, larger, softer balls are usually easier for little hands to handle.

202

whip up a smoothie

Let your toddler help you make a fruit shake with a handful of fruit (bananas and berries are especially good), a scoop of ice cream or frozen yogurt, and a splash of juice. Mix well in a blender, making sure there are no lumps that could cause choking. A smoothie makes a great breakfast!

203

show off some art

Chances are that your little artist is producing a multitude of artworks at this stage. One idea to help you showcase his creative outpouring is to buy magnetic sheets at a craft store and make refrigerator picture frames. Cut out concentric rectangles so that each becomes a slightly smaller frame—the tiniest one from the center can set off a particularly nice detail. Or use his masterworks to decorate his room. You can also scan some of your favorite pieces into your computer and e-mail them to friends and family, display them as your monitor's "wallpaper," or turn them into a digital slide show.

204

make designer shoelaces

Lay child-sized shoelaces on a paper towel and ask your child to help you add polka dots to them with nontoxic fabric paint (a pencil eraser makes a stamp of the right size). Once dry, lace them into her shoes.

205

be upwardly mobile

By now your child is probably getting pretty good at stair climbing, though going up is still easier than going down. He might still like to scoot downstairs on his bottom, one step at a time, or walk down wedding-march style, so that both feet are on the same step at the same time. To build his confidence, practice going up and down together, but when you're not practicing, keep the stairs in your home safely gated.

206

hop on a magic carpet

Cut the bottom out of a large paper grocery bag, then snip along one folded edge to make a large rectangle. Cut a fringe into the two ends, then help your child color designs on this "carpet" with nontoxic washable markers. Once he's aboard his carpet, fire up his powers of imagination by asking him what he sees below. "Are you flying over the house? Do you see the swing set? Is that Tessie barking in the backyard?"

207

invent some rhymes

Start by letting your child finish familiar rhyming phrases, then add new ones. Once the concept is understood, take turns adding to a list of words that rhyme, such as cat, mat, bat, hat, and rat.

208

"teach me to play nice...
Show me the fun I can
have when I share my toys
and play with other kids."

209

sniff it out

The nose knows, so ask your child to close her eyes, then stimulate her senses by asking her to sniff and identify safe kitchen items. Vanilla, cinnamon, and cocoa are good ones to try. Avoid peppers or spicy things that might irritate her nose or eyes.

210

paint a cookie canvas

Put a small amount of water in three bowls and add drops of food coloring to each bowl to create three different bright hues (the ratio of water to food coloring should be about two to one). Let your child use new, small paintbrushes to paint with these colors on unbaked sugar cookies. Once they're baked and cooled, let him eat his masterpieces.

POSTCARD

DEC 15
2006

CORRESPONDENCE

ADDRESS

_____

_____

_____

_____

211

make a mail call

Mail may seem like magic to a toddler. Buy a small
toy mailbox—or make one out of a shoe box—and
deliver notes or small toys to it from time to time.
Encourage friends and relatives to send postcards
to your child. Sort through your junk mail for
colorful envelopes to help fill her mailbox.

212

have a drum session

Set up a bunch of percussion "instruments" outside or in a playroom. Include anything you've got that can be safely tapped, banged, or pounded: oatmeal boxes, pots and pans, tin sand pails, blocks of wood, cookie tins, dishpans, and empty plastic milk bottles are good things to start with. Offer your little drummer boy some spoons (wood, metal, or plastic) or a wooden kitchen mallet, and belt out his favorite tunes while he provides the percussion. Or just sit back and enjoy his extended drum solo. He's not just having fun, he's also honing his sense of rhythm and eye-hand coordination.

213

get picky

Place a dozen or so light objects—marshmallows, feathers, cereal—into a dish in front of your child. Give her a pair of blunt tweezers and show her how to pick up the objects and move them to another dish. This is a great way to sharpen fine motor skills, but since small objects are involved, watch closely.

214

sort things out

Lay out a dozen similar items, such as large beads or buttons, and ask your child to sort them by color, shape, or size. Then have him sort by more subtle characteristics, like the number of holes in a button. Always be sure no small objects wind up in his mouth.

215

plant a carrot top

Cut the tops from a few whole carrots (parsnip and radish tops work, too—but not precut baby carrots) about 1 inch (2.5 cm) from the top. Help your toddler set them, cut side down, in a shallow dish. Pour in water until it's about halfway up the carrot tops. Continue to water and watch them every day. Soon feathery green leaves will reward your little gardener.

216

have a scavenger hunt

Give your child a magazine with lots of photos, then name a category—say, purple things, babies, food, or animals—and ask her to point out examples of those items as you page through the magazine with her.

217

draw out "hide and seek"

Don't be too quick to uncover the kid giggling behind the curtain or under the table. Instead, say aloud, "Wow, if only *[your child's name]* were here, he could tell me what a cow says." Keep the game going with different animals until he reveals himself—or is laughing so hard it's impossible to pretend you don't know where he's hiding.

218

eat some ants

Cut celery sticks into short lengths and spread cream cheese or hummus into the hollow of each stick. Have your toddler scatter raisin "ants" along the top of each piece. Who knew bugs could be so tasty?

219

grow by leaps and...jumps?

Games and challenges that involve jumping are great for two-year-olds. They promote gross motor development, fine-tune their balance, and increase agility. They're also a great outlet for all that toddler energy. So draw a series of stars, polka dots, or flowers with sidewalk chalk, and see whether your child can jump from one to the other with both feet together. Later on, she might want to try hopping on one foot, then the other, or even try out the classic childhood game of hopscotch.

220

make instant puppets

Looking for a way to amuse your child in a hurry?
Use a nontoxic pen to draw faces on the pads of his
index fingers. He can amuse himself by having his
two finger people talk to each other—and you!

221

create sponge art

Cut new kitchen sponges into strips and circles, let
your child dip them into a small puddle of nontoxic
liquid paint on a paper plate, and then press, drag,
or dab the sponges onto paper. A sponge rolled
into a tube and secured every 2 inches (5 cm) or so
with rubber bands leaves an unusual impression
when rolled across the paper. Try it out!

222

pack a picnic

Who cares if it's the same old cheese sandwich you were going to make for your toddler to eat at the kitchen table? And never mind that it's just in your backyard. Do your picnic up right—basket, checkered cloth, and plastic cups. Outdoors, the juice is juicier; the cheese, cheesier; the carrot sticks, crunchier. Lie back with your child and search for sharks, trains, and alligators in the clouds, and you're well on your way to a memorable afternoon.

223

" give me a break...
If I'm worked up, take me away from the scene. Let me suck my thumb or clutch my blanket—or just hold me. Your touch is magic. **"**

224

sing a song of sixpence

This short song has a lot packed into it—a royal cast of characters and a flock of naughty blackbirds.

Sing a song of sixpence,
A pocket full of rye.
Four-and-twenty blackbirds baked in a pie.
When the pie was opened, the birds began to sing,
And wasn't that a dainty dish to set before a king?
The king was in his counting house,
counting out his money.
The queen was in the parlor,
eating bread and honey.
The maid was in the garden,
hanging out the clothes.
When along came a blackbird
and nipped her on the nose!
gently tap your little one's nose

225

promote construction

Chances are your child is content with ordinary stacking blocks, but this is a good age to introduce new building toys. Look for toddler versions of construction logs and connecting blocks, ones that are sized for small hands and fingers, and safe to mouth and bite. Don't expect the Taj Mahal to rise on the playroom floor just yet. For now, the appeal is making things connect, and having them stay together for a while—long enough to show off to an admiring parent.

226

dine in style

Even your little one will enjoy fancy dinners at home
from time to time, and it allows him to become familiar
with more formal settings. Put out a tablecloth, let
him help with an arrangement of flowers, play soft
jazz or classical music in the background, and
a meal of macaroni and cheese becomes elegant.

227

explain change

Changes in your appearance can still be a little
startling for your two-year-old. A hat or a pair
of sunglasses might be fine, but if you were to
color your hair or cut it very differently she might
need some reassurance that it's really you.
Explain the changes, and she'll soon adapt.

228

get the blues

Once in a while, devote a day to a specific color.
If it's blue, for instance, dress in blue clothes, eat
blueberries, color with blue crayons, and play with blue
toys. Look for blue things wherever you go and make
a game of pointing them out to each other.

229

make a portable banana split

Here's a snack that you can make together. Ask
your toddler to peel a banana, then give it to you
to cut in half crosswise. Help your child roll the
banana sections in melted chocolate (make sure it
is cool enough for little hands!), insert a wooden
popsicle stick into each one for a handle, set
them on wax paper, and freeze them for a half hour.

230

eat what you read

Prepare and eat a food inspired by one of your child's favorite books. You could serve up a Dr. Seuss special of green eggs and ham, or Maurice Sendak's *Chicken Soup with Rice*. Or why not taste a little of Goldilocks' beloved porridge?

231

wear a little nature

Outfit your toddler with flowers and weeds: make a necklace from daisies or dandelions, or a crown of wild grasses and flowers. If you live near maple trees, look for the seed "wings," which, when split open and sticky, make a great rhino horn to adorn your child's nose.

232

shape some sandwiches

Use a cookie cutter or a knife to cut your child's sandwiches into interesting shapes. Or make a bicolored lunch by using one slice of white bread and one slice of whole wheat or pumpernickel.

233

set up a command center

Write simple directions on slips of paper (for instance, "turn around," "hop like a bunny," and "bring me your toy cat"). Let your child pull the directions out of a plastic jar one at a time, and read them out to him. See how many directions he can remember and follow at a time. Let him select some commands for you, too.

234

put on a shadow play

Shine a bright light on the wall of a darkened room, and make shadow-puppet animals with your hands, using them to act out stories. Then help your child create some easy-to-make animal shadows of his own. Two good ones to start with are a rabbit (just have him hold up his fingers to show how old he is) and a butterfly (ask him to spread the fingers of both hands, holding them so that his thumbs are touching).

235

sing "wheels on the bus"

Where did this song come from? No one seems
to know. But toddlers sure love to sing it.

The wheels on the bus go round and round,
Round and round,
Round and round.
The wheels on the bus go round and round,
All through the town.

There are countless additional verses.
Here are some favorites:

The doors on the bus go open and shut...
The driver on the bus says, "Move on back"...
The wipers on the bus go swish, swish, swish...
The horn on the bus goes beep, beep, beep...
The baby on the bus cries, "Waa, waa, waa"...
The mommy on the bus says, "Shh, shh, shh"...

236

savor world cuisine

Get your child used to eating all kinds of cuisines
early on. This will make it easier for your family to
enjoy a variety of taste sensations while broadening
her sensory experience. While a few toddlers happily
cut their teeth on Cajun-spiced pizza, most little ones
don't like strong tastes yet, so start with the milder
dishes: Chinese sesame noodles and sweet-and-sour
chicken, gently spiced Indian biryani (rice) and nan
(flat bread), or Middle Eastern hummus and falafel.
Expand your child's cultural horizons by talking to
him about the country the food comes from.

237

block out the pattern

Take eight toy blocks, four in each of two different colors. Lay out a pattern—say, two red blocks side by side. Give your toddler the remaining blocks and ask her to copy your model. Keep the game going by making a few more patterns for her to match.

238

sing to the moon

If you don't know the original tune to this traditional folk song, just improvise a melody.

I see the moon, and the moon sees me,
The moon sees somebody I'd like to see.
Bless the moon and bless me,
And bless somebody I'd like to see.

239

"treat my teddy with care... Wash my favorite plush toy if you must—but please do it when I'm asleep, and sneak him back into my bed before I wake up in the morning."

240

watch and encourage

Let your child take his time to work out new things,
such as solving a jigsaw puzzle. He's becoming more
self-reliant—and loves to be encouraged when he
succeeds. Step in only if he gets frustrated.

241

have fun with felt

Purchase a felt board or make one by covering a
large, sturdy piece of cardboard with felt from a fabric
store. Then buy some ready-made felt stick-ons, or cut
out your own from pieces of felt: geometric shapes,
animals, people, clouds, trees, airplanes, robots,
dinosaurs, or whatever your child is interested in. This
old-fashioned and low-tech way to design scenes and
tell stories is perfect for amusing a two-year-old.

242

make more of the shore

Take your toddler to the beach and help her find her sea legs. Let her feel the surf around her ankles, and carry her securely into the water, gently reassuring her if she's nervous. Back on shore, search for treasures, then sort them: shells, driftwood, and smooth sea glass—even creatures like periwinkles might find themselves in her bucket. Help her to gently examine the live things and return them to their original homes. If she finds trash, there's a lesson there, too—help her take it to the nearest garbage can.

243

go out in the rain

Go outside every day, unless the weather's truly nasty. In fact, rainy walks can be the best kind. Put on boots and slickers and linger over (and jump in) puddles, search for earthworms on the sidewalk, float leaves in little pools, and tip your heads back and catch raindrops on your tongues. Sometimes it's fun getting wet!

244

play "concentration"

Print out matching pictures from the Internet, lay them out face up (four pictures—two pairs—are enough to start with), then turn them face down and see if your child can turn over two that match. Add more pairs to keep the game challenging. Or try "Color Concentration," with pairs of colored cards, such as paint samples.

245

promote the chef

Let your toddler graduate to some real cooking duty. Supervise as he stirs up granola, tosses a salad, or uses a cookie cutter to shape dough. Make his *sous-chef* status official by giving him a pint-sized apron of his very own.

246

sing about a bear

Explore new heights with this adventurous tune:

The bear went over the mountain,
sing three times in a row

To see what he could see.

He saw another mountain;
sing three times in a row

It was all that he could see!

247

visit a farmers' market

An outing to a market is as fun as it is educational.
Invite your toddler to help you find the things you
want: "Can you help me pick out five apples?"
Buy something new to eat, and let her make some
choices of her own. Toddlers are more likely to
try things that they've had a hand in picking out.

248

run a car wash

Encourage your child's instinct to take care of his things by helping him gather his toy cars and trucks outside or in the bathtub for a clean-up. Give him a small pail of soapy water and a sponge so he can wash them, then help him rinse them. For safety, stay with him and empty the bucket when he's all done.

249

mess it up!

Your toddler will love it when she hears you make a mistake. Saying "Oh, hey, great red shirt!" when she's wearing blue, or confusing song lyrics ("Sing a song of sixpence, a pocket full of sky...") will crack her up and promote her cognitive and language development.

250

get ambitious with blocks

Your child's ability to build with blocks gets a lot more sophisticated during this period. She now has the fine motor skills to build taller towers and longer trains. Show her architectural tricks, like how to add spaces to toy-block constructions by straddling a cube across two slightly separated ones underneath.

251

design a private cave

Drape a blanket over a card table so that it covers all four sides to the ground, then tuck up one side to make a doorway. Presto: a perfect cave for one (or one toddler, two plush toys, three trucks, and a cookie). Throw in a blanket and a flashlight, and you've got deluxe toddler accommodations.

252

make eight-legged friends

Make an octopus doll out of an old clean sock. Stuff the toe end with cotton balls or quilt batting, then tie a short bit of string or yarn tightly under the stuffed section so it holds its round shape. Use scissors to cut fifteen slits from the cuff end of the sock to within 1 inch (2.5 cm) or so of the string. Add some eyes with a nontoxic marker.

253

play some water music

Fill six sturdy glasses with different amounts of water, arranging them from least full to most full. Show your child how to gently tap them with a metal spoon to make music. Demonstrate how adding or subtracting water changes the glasses' tones.

254

" help me be generous...
I'm starting to understand the joy
of giving—and I want to join in!
Teach me to share with other kids
or to make a present for a friend. **"**

255

make a puzzling sandwich

Cut your child's sandwich into two or three irregular pieces. Challenge him to put the puzzle pieces back together—then reward himself by eating the sandwich.

256

have a night out

When your toddler's up past dark, go out in the yard. Spread out a blanket (snuggle under another one if it's chilly), let your eyes adjust to the darkness, and talk about the moon and stars. Sing "Twinkle, Twinkle, Little Star" or "Fly Me to the Moon." Listen to the crickets, frogs, and any night birds that live in your area. Keep your eyes peeled for lightning bugs!

257

make some dough

Delight your child by making your own playing dough.

3 cups flour
1½ cups salt
6 teaspoons cream of tartar
3 tablespoons vegetable oil
3 cups water
Few drops of food coloring in three colors

Combine all the ingredients except the food coloring in a large pot over medium heat. Stir constantly until the mixture pulls away from the sides of the pot and forms a ball. Remove from the heat and allow to cool. Once cool enough to handle, turn dough onto waxed paper and knead it for a minute or so. Then divide it into three portions and knead in the food colorings to make each a different color. The dough is now ready for your child to play with. Store each dough portion in separate bags in the refrigerator. Discard after a week or two.

258

hop the animal train

Make a train by poking a small hole in each end
of several shoe boxes and tying them together with
yarn or ribbon. Let your child be the conductor of
the Animal Express and, with her whistle blowing,
help her load up her toys for a ride.

259

share musical memories

Let your toddler hear the music of your own
childhood. Dig out your old recordings or find some
CDs of the songs you once listened to. You'll be
astonished at how many of the songs you can still
sing—and who knows, you may keep the musical
tradition going for another generation.

260

bake a snake cake

Bake a cake in a Bundt pan; when it's cool, cut
it into three pieces. Ask your child to help you arrange
them on a platter so the curves form a slithering snake.
Frost with green frosting, and let your toddler help you
add cherry eyes and some sugar-wafer spots.

261

blow a harmonica

A harmonica is a great instrument for toddlers
because it makes noise whether they inhale or exhale.
Blowing up and down the edge of the harmonica
helps them learn about musical scales, too.

262

make bubbles

Pour bubble mix into a wide dish and demonstrate how to blow bubbles with a bubble wand, or shape your own from a pipe cleaner or toilet tissue tube (these get soggy after a while, so have a few on hand). Dip a plastic berry basket in the soapy soup and wave it to make dozens of tiny bubbles.

263

inspire a budding author

Your child may be starting to show an interest in writing by pretending to write. Encourage her, but don't worry about teaching the mechanics of writing just yet. Give her crayons and paper, and then ask her to read you what she's "written."

24+

24 months & up

264

play "i spy" with your ears

Say, "I hear, with my little ear, two noises that are pretty near!" Ask your child to tell you two things she hears: a dog barking and a plane passing overhead, for instance. Make the game more challenging by asking for specifics, such as "I hear something that you ride in—what is it?"

265

try a coat trick

Putting on a coat can be hard for kids, so try this method: help your child lay his jacket, unbuttoned and faceup, on the floor in front of him so that the collar opening is at his feet. Guide him as he bends over and inserts his arms into the sleeves, then help him flip the coat over his head so that it lands in the right position when he finishes putting his arms through the sleeves.

266

capture your child's day

Take photos of your child throughout the day, doing what he likes to do: playing, eating, going for walks, exploring the yard, picking up a sibling at school, helping out at home, and so on. Print or paste these pictures onto sheets of paper you can make into a booklet, or slide them into an album. It's guaranteed to become one of your toddler's very favorite books.

267

sing "london bridge"

Now's a good time to introduce simple musical rhymes and games that two or more people can play together. Two children (or adults) join hands to make the bridge under which the kids march as you sing. At "my fair lady," of course, one child is caught under the bridge and swayed gently during the chorus, then let go.

London Bridge is falling down,
Falling down, falling down.
London Bridge is falling down,
My fair lady.

[Chorus] *Take a key and lock her up,*
Lock her up, lock her up.
Take a key and lock her up,
My fair lady.

268

dine with a worm

At a restaurant, create a friendly "worm" dining companion. Slip two drinking straws from their wrappers. Lay the end of one wrapper over the end of the other so that they form an L shape, and fold the one on the bottom over the one on top. Repeat, continuing to alternate folds until both wrappers are completely folded up. You'll have an accordion-like critter that can amuse your little one with its antics. No wrapped straws? Use paper strips from a napkin.

269

play a color game

Expand your toddler's knowledge of color by laying out paper in bright crayon shades. Ask him to match crayons to the papers as you both name the colors.

270

be a patron of the arts

For a two-year-old, drawing is more about the physical act than making a design that represents a flower or a person. Praise her for what she's doing and how much fun she's having doing it. Still, it's fine to interpret a little: "Wow, that looks like an apple to me—it's so beautiful!"

271

ride on a train

Line up the chairs in the dining room and invite your toddler—and any other family members who want to come along—to jump aboard the Chair Express, the fastest train in the house. Let him hand out construction paper "tickets" and collect them as riders get off and on.

272

set sail for animal island

The sofa is the boat, and the floor is Animal Island. If you disembark, you become an animal and must talk and move like a wild creature. Got something you have to say? Get back in the boat so you can communicate like a human being again.

30+

from thirty months & up

As your little one nears the end of his toddler months, he's becoming very much his own person, with his unique talents, gifts, and opinions. The speed at which toddlers pick up new skills and information can leave you breathless at times, and there's no easing of the pace as he nears his third birthday. This is a golden age, with much of the willfulness of earlier toddler times making way for more relaxed interactions. You're still his favorite guide to his rapidly expanding world, so take time to enjoy this special stage together.

273

head down to the farm

Working farms that are open to visitors are worth searching out. Or perhaps you've noticed a place near you where animals graze in the fields. And a petting zoo with lambs and goats can seem quite exotic to city toddlers. Once you've found a suitable place, give your child a chance to see live versions of the animals in his storybooks. Wear boots, and always ask permission before attempting to pet or feed an animal. Wash your hands well afterward.

274

create fingerprint friends

Put out a pad of nontoxic washable ink (or nontoxic
liquid paint on a paper plate) and ask your child to
make fingerprints or thumbprints on paper. Once
they're dry, use a marker to add details such as legs,
tails, and petals to create people, animals, or flowers.

275

balance on a ball

Stimulate your child's sense of balance with a large
vinyl "hopping" ball with a handle (sold at toy shops
and sporting-goods stores). Although her feet may not
yet touch the ground when she's on the ball, she can
still sit and hold the handle. Bounce the ball gently
with one hand, keeping her upright with the other.

276

use the power of nonsense

When your child is feeling off his game, challenge him to look you straight in the eye and very slowly say "cabbage, cabbage, cabbage" without laughing or cracking a smile. Almost impossible!

277

shake a rain stick

Scrunch a 5-foot (1.5-m) long piece of aluminum foil into the shape of a snake, then coil it into a spiral that fits inside an empty cardboard gift-wrap tube. Securely seal one end of the tube with heavy paper and packing tape. Pour ⅔ cup dried lentils into the open end, then securely seal that end, too. Stand the stick upright and listen to the "rain."

278

"let's look at our feet... It helps me develop pride in my body if you show me that I am the same as you, as well as unique.**"**

279

build a fairy home

Go looking for fairy houses with your little one—are they under a twisted tree root, beneath the edge of the back step, inside a tangle of summer flowers? Bring the fairies a flat piece of bark for a table, moss for their beds, and acorn caps of water to drink. To help them upgrade their lodgings, use twigs, leaves, and other natural materials to build them a new home.

280

get heavy

"Heavy" work is great for developing your child's gross motor skills, and the accomplishment builds her self-esteem. So offer her a small pile of clothes to take to the closet or a sturdy bag to carry her books from one room to another.

281

cook up crazy crayons

Got lots of broken crayon bits? Line a muffin pan with paper liners. Peel the labels off the crayons and sort them, say, with all the blue shades in one cup and all the metallics in another. Fill the muffin cups one-third full, then bake at 225°F (110°C), watching closely, until the bits have melted. Let cool, peel off the liners, and then invite your child to use these crazy crayons.

282

play mad scientist

Spread newspapers on a table and give your little chemist bowls of water, spoons, empty plastic cups, and cups containing a little salt, sugar, flour, lemon juice, or water. Let her mix, concoct, stir, and taste, expanding her sensory knowledge of the world.

283

sing a song of shrubbery

Enjoy the classic version, then adapt this song to other activities, like, "This is the way we pet the cat."

Here we go 'round the mulberry bush,
The mulberry bush, the mulberry bush.
Here we go 'round the mulberry bush
So early in the morning.

284

turn shopping into a game

To hone his matching skills, hand your child coupons and ask him to watch out for the items shown while he's sitting in the grocery cart. Offer hints like "I think you'll find that one in this aisle."

285

admire the ducks

Pay a visit to a duck pond to introduce your toddler to some feathered friends. See how many different kinds of ducks you can spot. If you sit quietly, they'll probably get comfortable with you and your child. With luck, they'll come close so you can get a good look—and a good listen to their quacks. Invite her to imitate the ducks by doing a bit of quacking herself.

286

try out a different "i spy"

Play "I Spy" with a twist by focusing on what things do. For instance, you might say, "I spy something that plays music" (or that you can ride in, eat with, or sit on). It's a fun way to teach your child how things work.

287

put on a new face

Help your toddler place a medium-sized paper bag over his head, and gently use a crayon to mark where his eyes and mouth are. Take the bag off and cut openings at the marked spots. Set him up with crayons, nontoxic liquid paint, paper cutouts, and nontoxic glue so he can transform his new face into his wildest fancy, be it a tiger, a robot, or an alien.

288

teach scissor savvy

Toward the end of their third year, some children may be able to cut paper with scissors. To encourage the development of that fine motor skill, make sure that the scissors are child-safe but not so dull that they result in a frustrating experience. Teach your child from the beginning that scissors are to be used only with an adult around and only while seated. Help your little artist by giving her crisp paper (like construction paper) and holding the sides taut while she cuts fringe on an edge. As her skill develops, cut out strips for her to cut into squares, and then help her glue them onto colored paper to make a design.

289

sprout some initials

Help your child dampen a pad of cotton batting and lay it in a dish. Sprinkle wheat seeds in the shape of his initials on the cotton and help him keep them moist until they sprout and his initials come to life!

290

be penny-wise

Demonstrate some fun chemistry by dropping dirty pennies into a glass jar with a lid. Cover them with vinegar, then throw in a tablespoon of salt. Seal the jar and shake gently. Help your child shake the jar again once or twice later on, and those pennies will be clean by the next day. Remind her that no matter how shiny, pennies should never go in mouths.

291

try out your spanish

Your child probably knows all the words to "Head, Shoulders, Knees, and Toes." Now try it in Spanish!

Cabeza, hombros, rodillas y pies
Rodillas y pies!
Cabeza, hombros, rodillas y pies
Rodillas y pies!
Ojos, orejas, boca y nariz.
Cabeza, hombros, rodillas y pies
Rodillas y pies!

292

teach about opposites

Ask your toddler to name the opposite of the word you say. Start with easy ones: girl, boy; on, off; big, small.

293

mix some colors

Put nontoxic liquid paint in the three primary
colors (red, blue, yellow) on a painter's palette
or around the edges of a plate. Demonstrate
how combining two colors creates a new one.

294

get boxed in

Call an appliance store and ask if a large cardboard
box can be saved for you—one that originally
contained an oven or a refrigerator. With a box knife
(in your hands) and crayons (in your child's), the
box can become a grocery store, a puppet theater,
a puppy kennel, or a castle. With the right props, his
imagination can conjure up limitless possibilities.

295

use your noggin

Kids love figuring out which item in a series doesn't fit with the rest. At this stage, you can help hone your child's logical thinking by making things harder. For instance, show her a sneaker, a flip-flop, a sock, and a boot. The odd item might be the sock, because it's not a shoe. Or maybe it's the flip-flop, since you only wear it in the summer. The reasoning behind the answer is as interesting as the answer itself.

296

make a paper-bag doll

Loosely stuff a paper lunch bag with newspaper. Seal this round "head" with tape, and attach a torso, arms, and legs cut out of construction paper. Ask your child to draw a face on her floppy new friend.

297

"respect my blankie...
When I want to comfort myself,
it reminds me of things that are
warm and snuggly (like you),
and helps me to hang in there."

30+

30 months & up

298

collaborate on a book

Your toddler is full of stories, so team up on a book: he dictates; you write; he illustrates. Put just a few lines of text on each page, leaving plenty of room for artwork. Once you finish the book, bind his masterpiece in construction paper, then ask him to add some cover art and choose a title.

299

make cleaning a game

When child's play turns into a major mess, enlist your toddler in a cleanup—but make it fun. Ask her to clean up all the red things, or all the square things. Or play "take 10": set out a timer and see how much she can tidy in 10 minutes, or ask her to put away 10 items—and then maybe 10 more.

300

play crayon-box bingo

On your next road trip, give your child a small box of fat crayons and use them to improve his color sense. Ask him to watch the cars you pass, and when he spots a red one, to hand you the red crayon, and so on. When the box is empty, he's won!

301

explore snackitecture

Serve up a plate of snacks that double as building supplies: cheese cut into cubes, peeled apple pieces, cut-up grapes, marshmallows, and pretzel sticks. See what sorts of structures your child makes out of these building materials before she gobbles them up.

302

clap for miss mack

Enjoy this classic clapping rhyme any time. Face your toddler and mark the rhythm of the words "Mack, Mack, Mack" each time they're sung by clapping on your knees, or clapping your hands against your child's. Start slowly and see how fast you can get.

Miss Mary Mack, Mack, Mack,
All dressed in black, black, black,
Had silver buttons, buttons, buttons
All down her back, back, back.

She asked her mother, mother, mother
For fifty cents, cents, cents,
To see the elephant, elephant, elephant
Jump over the fence, fence, fence.

It jumped so high, high, high,
It reached the sky, sky, sky.
And it didn't come back, back, back
'Til the fourth of July, July, July!

303

make dandelion wishes

Teach your child how to make a wish and blow the seeds off a ripe dandelion head. Use a magnifying glass to study the structure of the individual seeds. Then pretend he's a dandelion: make a wish out loud, blow on his hair, and encourage your little seedling to spin across the yard.

30+

304

assemble a car kit

Purchase an inexpensive metal baking pan, the kind with a plastic lid that slides on and off. Use the pan to store felt cutouts of geometric shapes, people, animals, trees, clouds, and so on—all great for imaginative play. Add a drawing pad, crayons, and large magnetic letters (which can be used on the bottom of the pan). Adapt the kit to your child's interests by including her favorite diversions, be they dinosaurs, puppets, or books. When you're hitting the road, throw in a few healthy snacks such as granola bars or boxes of raisins.

305

whip up a parfait

Let your toddler make a healthy fruit sundae in
a tall plastic parfait glass. Help her layer yogurt,
sliced strawberries or other berries, and something
crunchy, like crumbled graham crackers. She'll
enjoy making it almost as much as eating it.

306

set the table

Help your child make paper cutouts of a plate,
knife, spoon, fork, and glass (you may need to do
most of the cutting). Together, glue them into their
proper places on a construction-paper place mat.
Take the paper place setting to the copy shop
and have it laminated so your little helper can
use it as a model every time he sets the table.

30+

30 months & up

307

enjoy a concert

Toddlers love outdoor concerts, especially ones geared
to kids. Bring a blanket or some folding chairs, a picnic,
and a pillow and a plush toy in case the concert is a
snooze. If it's lively, though, let her run around and
dance as the spirit moves her, as long as she doesn't
stray too far from home base—and your sight.

308

experiment with magnets

Magnets are wonderful toys for discovery play. Visit
the hardware store and purchase a variety of large
magnets—rods, horseshoes, and circles. Don't be
too quick to explain the principles of magnetism to
your child—he'll discover them himself (and have
more fun) by playing with them. Do explain that
because magnets are not kind to watches, cell phones,
speakers, or computers, they should be kept away from
these items—and that they never belong in his mouth!

309

make an impression

Potato prints are always a hit with kids. Cut a
potato in half, and cut out a shape. Put out nontoxic
liquid paint, and let your child make her mark.

310

"help me find myself...
It will be years before
my interests firm up, so
it's great to try out lots
of new things now.**"**

311

make edible initials

Buy an inexpensive set of letter-shaped cookie cutters, and use them to cut out your child's name or initials from a piece of cinnamon toast or a grilled cheese sandwich. Yummy (and secretly educational)!

312

get creative with chalk

Carry some colorful sidewalk chalk in your car. Most park and school groundskeepers are tolerant about the use of chalk since the next rain will wash the marks away, anyway. Draw lily pads, so your little frog can hop from one to another. Make square "pages," and tell a story in words or pictures. Don't worry if the pavement's damp; colored chalks are at their most brilliant when wet.

313

try some tongue twisters

See if your child can get his mouth around these:

Toy boat, toy boat, toy boat, toy boat.

Or:

She sells seashells by the seashore.

Or this one:

Three gray geese in the green grass grazing.

314

bake watermelon slices

Make crunchy slices of "watermelon" by using red food coloring to tint chocolate-chip cookie dough. Have your child help you shape dough into a roll and dip its edge in diluted green food coloring. Slice into semicircles. Bake and munch away.

315

trace some leaves

Have your toddler collect a handful of leaves from your yard or the park. Then set out a few crayons without their wrappers and some medium-weight paper (plain copy paper works well). Lay the leaves facedown (veiny side up) on the table and put the paper on top of them. Help your child stroke evenly over the leaf with the broad side of a crayon, revealing the leaf's image on the paper. Have her try using the same technique with other textured and relatively flat items like tree bark, a fossil in a rock, or the whorl of seeds in the center of a sunflower. Make a mobile by cutting out several of her favorite rubbings, punching a hole in the top of each and using thread to tie them along a chopstick or a dowel.

30+

30 months & up

316

pick a peck

Check your local papers for "pick-your-own" farms
that let families harvest produce. This is usually fruit,
but some farms also offer beans, corn, or pumpkins.
Fill your baskets together when you're in the fields,
then pay and wash before you eat. Get on the farm's
mailing list in your child's name: he'll be tickled to
get a postcard telling him that the pumpkins are
ripe and ready for him to choose!

317

walk the plank

Lay a sturdy 2-by-6-inch (5-by-15-cm) board or narrow table leaf that's about 3 feet (90 cm) long on two thick phone books, one under each end, so the board is roughly level and about 4 inches (10 cm) off the ground. Guide your child as she practices walking across it. Once she's mastered that, give her sense of balance a real workout by trying it backward!

318

get scientific in the bath

Scrunch a dry washcloth into the bottom of a large plastic cup. Help your child submerge the cup in the water, open end first, then raise it straight up again. Turn it over, and ask him to check the cloth. Discuss how it can be dry when it was under the water.

319

plant a box garden

You can use an actual window box, or just lay a milk carton on its side and cut off the uppermost side. Add some potting soil and help your child plant a few quick-to-grow seeds (zinnia, marigold, grass, and beans are all good choices). When the soil begins to feel dry, water it together. This is a good opportunity to start using a calendar, too—note the date on which you planted the seeds and help your child check off the days until the first sprouts appear.

320

express puppy love

Singing about a new dog is almost as much fun as having one.

How much is that doggie in the window,
The one with the waggly tail?
How much is that doggie in the window,
I do hope that doggie's for sale.

I don't want a fluffy little kitten;
I don't want a parrot that talks.
I don't want a bowl of little fishies;
You can't take a fish for a walk.

I just want that doggie in the window,
The one with the waggly tail.
How much is that doggie in the window?
I do hope that doggie's for sale!

321

grow a vine

Buy a sweet potato or a yam. (Bring home
some extras to eat: baked for an hour at 400°F,
or 200°C, yams make a healthy and naturally
sweet toddler treat.) Holding the uncooked yam
upright, stick in four toothpicks around the
center so that it will rest in the mouth of a jar
with about half sticking out the top. Add water
to the jar until it's about halfway up the yam,
and set the jar in a sunny spot. Ask your child
to help you top off the water level if it dips. It
may take a week or two for the yam to sprout,
but once it does, it will grow rapidly. Soon
you'll have a lush vine—and your child will
have a better appreciation of nature's magic.

322

play a xylophone

Buy a small xylophone, the kind with metal keys that are often used in grade schools. It will last forever, and your child will have a great time just puttering with it. And she'll sharpen her eye-hand coordination and develop her musical ear while she's at it!

323

teach about time

Old-fashioned analog clocks, especially those with sweeping second hands, often fascinate toddlers. Talk about how the face of the clock is a circle, point out the big hand and the little hand, and count out the numbers—reminding him that the little hand should be on the "7" before he gets out of bed in the morning.

30+

30 months & up

324

test the tastebuds

Try this sensory-exploration game when you're in the kitchen. Have your little one close her eyes tightly and open her mouth. Pop something yummy in, then see if she can guess what it is. A piece of banana? A chocolate chip? Now ask her to hold her nose and try again—what differences does she notice?

325

draw some finger actors

Create instant puppets by cutting the fingers off a white cotton glove and putting them on your child's fingers. Use nontoxic cloth markers to draw faces and other features on them to help bring the "characters" to life. Make a whole cast of fanciful folk, then let your toddler make up his own drama.

326

"be my home base...
I'm trying out my independence,
and may wander away, but I'll
usually come back on my own.
Keep an eye on me, though."

327

create art central

Stock a small chest of drawers or a bookcase with open bins containing child-friendly art materials, and your toddler will always have the tools to express her creative side. Include copy paper, newspaper, construction paper, scraps of gift wrap, and sheets of cardboard. Add plastic boxes of "found" objects such as ribbons, yarn, wooden spools, extra large buttons, and popsicle sticks for making collages and other craft projects. Keep an "Ask First!" box of art supplies like nontoxic liquid paints, markers, and crayons—a repository for items she can use only with an adult's help or supervision—nearby but safely out of reach.

328

guess what's in the basket

Even an older toddler may not be ready for something as abstract as "20 Questions," but if you put a familiar object in a basket and cover it with a cloth, she might be able to guess what it is with a few hints. Then let her put something in the basket and challenge you to guess the mystery item's identity.

329

make a "bunny" salad

Show your child that making food can be fun. Ask him to put a clean lettuce leaf on a plate, then top it with a peeled pear half, cut side down. Give him two thin slices of baby carrots to stick into the pear's narrow end to make bunny ears. Add raisin eyes, a sliver of cherry for a nose, and a dollop of yogurt for a tail.

330

take in a movie

Sitting through a "real" movie in a big, dark theater might be a little demanding for a toddler. Instead, look for showings of short children's films at a local library or a community center. Or have family movie night at home with a DVD or a video.

331

get artsy

Collect the raw materials for a sculpture: wooden spools, empty milk cartons, and clean popsicle sticks, for example. Then let your budding artist loose with nontoxic craft glue. Chances are your child will be more of an abstract expressionist than a realist but at this age, most of the joy (and fine motor skill development) comes from just manipulating the shapes.

332

enjoy a jumpy rhyme

By now, your child might be too old for knee-bouncing rhymes. Then again, she might not!

Five little monkeys jumping on the bed.
One rolled off and bumped his head.
Mama called the doctor and the doctor said,
[Sternly] *"No more monkeys jumping on the bed!"*

for subsequent verses, count down until you reach "one little monkey"

One little monkey jumping on the bed.
She rolled off and bumped her head.
Mama called the doctor and the doctor said,
"No more monkeys jumping on the bed!"

333

play pizza parlor

Kids love doing things that reflect the grown-up world, so let your child try his hand as a pizza chef. Cut the "ingredients" for a pizza from felt: tan dough, maroon pepperoni, gray mushrooms, green peppers, and white cheese. Complete the effect with a few pizza boxes bought at your local real-life parlor. Throw in an apron so your little chef can serve his creation in style. *Buon appetito!*

334

make instant friends

Introducing...the foolproof origami puppy! Fold a square of paper in half, corner to corner, so it makes a triangle. With the folded edge of the paper facing away from you on the table, fold down the two outer corners so they look like floppy ears. Use a crayon or a pen to add eyes and a nose, and you've made a new buddy for your child. Make a whole litter of puppies, which your child can decorate with spots or stripes.

335

study the world of ants

Sprinkle sugar on the ground near an anthill, then give your child a plastic magnifier and let him spy on the ants as they gather their treasure. Do the ants seem to have different jobs? Are they a good team?

336

start a collection

Help your child explore her interests through collecting. A beach trip might spark a shell collection, a trip to the park a rock collection. Or maybe she always brings back the same type of souvenir from family vacations: a T-shirt or a snow globe. Whatever she collects, help her display her keepsakes, perhaps in clear plastic jars or boxes on an open shelf.

337

string some snacks

Let your toddler make an edible necklace by threading O-shaped cereal pieces, pretzels, and other stringable treats on twine or kitchen string.

338

belt out a funny tune

Older toddlers relish the sophisticated
wordplay of this venerable kids' song.

I knew a man called Michael Finnegan;
He had whiskers on his chinnegan.
They fell out and then grew in again,
Poor old Michael Finnegan.
Begin again!

339

make a personal puzzle

Glue one of your child's drawings onto cardboard
and cut it into a variety of shapes for him to fit
together. Or purchase a blank jigsaw puzzle and
have him draw on it, take it apart, and reassemble it.

340

"money's a bit of a mystery... But it's not too soon to get me started on saving. Help me count my coins—and maybe buy a treat with them!**"**

341

map it

Teaching basic map skills stretches your child's cognitive skills and spatial awareness, and it will help her get her bearings in your neighborhood. Grab a drawing pad and take a walk with your toddler on your street. Take a bird's-eye view: "If we were flying, what would we see next to our house when we looked down from the sky? Right, we'd see your friend Susan's house. What else would we see?" Sketch the street and draw boxes labeled "My House," "Susan's House," and "Playground," for example. When you get home, cut out simple construction-paper versions of these landmarks and see whether your child can help you place them in the right order. "Remember what came next? Was it the library or the hardware store?"

342

construct a riding route

If your toddler is ready to ride a tricycle, help him to gain skill on his new wheels by using sidewalk chalk to chart a course for him to follow in an unoccupied paved area. Include turns, loops, and stop signs. He'll relish the challenge—and his newfound mobility.

343

team up to make dinner

Divide homemade or store-bought pizza dough into fist-size balls and pat them thin and round. Set out bowls of tomato sauce, shredded cheese, olives, pepperoni slices—whatever your family enjoys on a pizza. Ask your toddler to take the family's orders for personal pizzas and let her arrange the desired toppings. You can take it from there.

344

look underwater

Make a viewing scope so your young marine biologist
can study the shallow water at the beach or a pond.
Cut both ends off a milk carton, cover one end with
tautly stretched plastic wrap, and tape the edges to
the sides of the carton with waterproof tape. Hold your
child while he submerges the plastic-covered end into
water and peeks through the other end. Hello, fish!

345

be an answer person

This age ushers in an explosion of endless
questions. Answer them as patiently as possible
since they're the way your child is expanding
his vocabulary and learning about the world.

346

root for the home team

Believe it or not, the man who wrote this classic American sports tune had never been to a baseball game. Your child, on the other hand, would love to go to one, even if you just head down to the park to see the local kids play. You can sing this on the way there:

Take me out to the ball game,
Take me out with the crowd.
Buy me some peanuts and Cracker Jack;
I don't care if I never get back!
Let me root, root, root for the home team;
If they don't win, it's a shame.
For it's one, two, three strikes, you're out,
At the old ball game!

347

tie-dye socks

Put a half-dozen pennies or marbles in one of your child's white cotton athletic socks, then do the same with its mate. Gather the fabric around each object to form a lump and tie each lump off with a string or a rubber band. Mix fabric dye in a bucket (disposable paper buckets are available in the paint department of hardware stores), and let your child drop them in. Submerge the socks, following the directions on the dye packet. Rinse the socks well, then dry them in a warm dryer. Untie the strings and have your child model her tie-dyed socks—guaranteed to please even the most style-conscious toddler.

30+

30 months & up

348

put together a dress-up kit

Kids love playing dress-up, and they don't need much encouragement to imagine themselves as bus drivers, animals, or magicians. Gather up old Halloween costumes, dress shirts, jackets, purses (ideally, complete with a wallet and business cards), and whatever other clothes and accessories you can donate to the cause. You'll be surprised at how much magic there is in your old winter hat!

349

whip up oobleck

Are you and your toddler ready for some messy science? Set yourself up—either outdoors or on a newspaper-covered kitchen table—with a wide plastic pan, two boxes of cornstarch, a pitcher of water you've tinted with food coloring, and a wooden spoon. Pour the cornstarch into the pan, and slowly stir in just enough water to make a mixture that's roughly the texture of cookie dough. You've just made Oobleck! Now let your child roll up her sleeves and play with it (you dive in there, too). Gather up a handful and squeeze it into a hard ball, then open your hand and watch it dribble back into ooze.

Note: don't pour Oobleck down the drain! When you're done, dispose of it by pouring it into an old milk carton and discarding it in the trash.

350

shine some starlight

Find an illustration of a simple constellation, such as Orion or the Big Dipper, in an astronomy book or online. Use a skewer or a small nail to poke holes in the bottom of a paper cup to correspond to the constellation's shape. At bedtime, darken your child's room and let him shine a flashlight through the holes in the cup to project "stars" on the ceiling.

351

create carton critters

To make a bug menagerie, cut a cardboard egg carton into pieces that have different numbers of cup-shaped sections. Punch some holes in strategic places, then invite your child to fashion brightly colored pipe cleaners into legs, antennae, and wings. A one-cup section might become a ladybug; a three-cup piece makes a great caterpillar.

352

play parking lot

Arrange pieces of colored construction paper "parking spaces" in a line and help your child "drive" toy cars onto them. Ask her to park each car on the colored square that matches it. Then mix up your instructions: "Please park the yellow truck in the red parking place."

353

visit the playground

Many school playgrounds are open to the public on weekends and school holidays, and they have far more equipment for climbing, swinging, and exploring than you're likely to have in your own backyard. So visit a few elementary schools, ones with playgrounds geared to the needs of smaller children. After trying out a few, give your child a choice: "Would you rather go to the playground with the pretend castle or the one with the giant turtle in the sandbox?" Don't forget to take snacks and drinks along on your adventure.

354

" **play with numbers...**
In a store or on the
street, stop a moment
and say, 'I spy something
with a number 3.' Then
praise me when I find it!**"**

355

shake a bit of butter

This is a good family or group activity, since the shaking can take a long time and goes much faster if you take turns. Fill a plastic jar that has a tight-fitting lid with very cold heavy cream until it's two-thirds full. Drop in two or three clean glass marbles to help mix the cream, then start shaking the jar briskly. You can recite this old rhyme to help pass the time:

Come, butter, come,
Come, butter, come.
Baby's standing at the gate,
Waiting for a butter cake.
Come, butter, come!

Switch back and forth, taking over from your toddler when he gets tired or bored. In 10 to 15 minutes, the cream will turn to butter. Strain out any remaining liquid, and use a wooden spoon to mix in salt to taste. Try your homemade butter on toast or crackers.

356

read to the dog

Budding readers may not know all the words in a
familiar picture book, but the dog doesn't know that.
So sit her down with Fido and let her "read" to him.
This activity works with cats or toy animals, too!

357

decorate snazzy cupcakes

Bake some cupcakes, then ask your toddler to help you try out these fun decorating ideas:

Add red food coloring to white frosting and use it to make the cupcakes look like apples. Let your child add a pretzel stem.

Tint the frosting blue, frost the cupcake, then sprinkle half of it with crushed vanilla wafer crumbs: sea and sand, just like the beach!

Turn a white-frosted cupcake into a baseball by painting on stitches with black frosting.

358

make a puppet theater

Hem 3 feet (90 cm) or so of fabric by folding the
top 2 inches (5 cm) down and stitching it in place.
Thread a tensioned curtain rod through the hem,
and position the rod horizontally in a doorway,
about 3 feet (90 cm) or so from the floor. Provide lots of
different kinds of puppets and props to make it
fun and interesting. Voilà—instant puppet theater!

359

get your potatoes out

To keep things fair in your toddler's group games,
demonstrate the time-honored method of determining
who goes first. Have all the children present extend
their fisted "potatoes," and count around using the
song "One Potato, Two Potato..." to decide who is first.

360

coach your toddler

New challenges sometimes leave your toddler feeling a little frustrated. Try these four steps to help him master a new task, be it zipping up his coat, pouring milk, or putting on socks:

1. Get his attention, then demonstrate and explain the task in simple language.

2. Give him materials that make the task easier—say, a big zipper pull, or a small pitcher into which you can pour the milk before he tries to pour it into his glass.

3. Break the task into steps to make it easier: "Look, scrunch up the top of the sock first, like this."

4. Give him encouraging feedback: "You did that part just right—now pull the zipper up a little higher, and you've got it!"

361

make some tiny friends

If you greet bugs and insects with happy surprise and curiosity, your child will do the same. Watch butterflies in the garden together, and let caterpillars walk on your hands. Show caution, not fear, around potentially stinging insects like bees, and your child will learn not to panic at the sight of them.

362

ride through the car wash

After your child has watched the family car go through the car wash a few times, see whether he'd like to ride inside the car with you as it goes through its soapy shower. Don't push it if he finds the idea a bit scary, but if he'd like to try it, explain that it will be a little noisy, and narrate everything that's happening.

30+

30 months & up

363

try out some humor

Jolly your child out of a bad mood by breaking into song—this classic usually does the trick.

Nobody likes me, everybody hates me,
I'm going to the garden to eat worms!
Nobody likes me, everybody hates me,
Going to the garden to eat worms!
Big fat slimy ones, little bitty skinny ones,
I'm going to the garden to eat worms!

364

design yourself

Take sidewalk chalks to a playground or your driveway. Have your child lie on his back, and trace his outline. Then give him the chalks so he can "dress" the figure and add realistic or fantastic facial features.

365

hang out in the diner

Even your toddler likes to go where somebody knows her name—and what she'd like for breakfast. So make a regular diner date with your little one, say, every Saturday morning. Let her order something she doesn't regularly eat at home. Chat with the servers, linger over milk and coffee, and leave a nice tip so they'll be happy to see the two of you again next week!

30+

30 months & up

index
a, b, c

"Airplane" rides, 23
Airplanes, 51
Alphabet, singing, 176
Ants, 27, 218, 335
"The Ants Go Marching One by
    One," 27
Art appreciation, 203, 270, 327
Balls, 89, 143, 201, 275
Beaches, 90, 95, 242, 344
"The Bear Went Over the Mountain,"
    246
Bedtime, 36, 45, 60, 65, 76, 131, 350
Bells, 116
Birds, 132, 187
Biting, 78
Blankets, 16, 251, 297
Blocks, 29, 135, 145, 225, 237, 250
Body awareness, 52, 103, 278
Book bags, 134
Books, 11, 57, 64, 82, 97, 109, 140, 146,
    184, 230, 298, 356
Boxes, 149, 294
Bubbles, 88, 122, 262
Bugs, 50, 124, 351, 361
"Bunny" salad, 329
Buses, 127, 235
Butter, 355
Cakes, 260
Car
    rides, 9, 93, 300, 304, 362
    toys, 248, 352
Carts, 67
Chalk, 312, 364
Change, 227
Choices, offering, 114, 125
Chores, 19, 32, 120, 121, 183, 280, 299
Climbing, 53
"The Clock Stands Still," 94
Clothes, 110, 166, 171, 265, 347
Coaching, 360
Collections, 336
Colors, 192, 228, 269, 293, 300

Comforting, 10, 108, 174, 223, 297
Commands, following, 96, 233
Cookies, 210, 314
Counting, 2, 56, 199, 332, 340
Crayons, 73, 141, 192, 281, 300, 315
Crowns, 37
Cupcakes, 357
Cushions, 53, 74, 137

d, e, f

Dandelion wishes, 303
Dinosaurs, 155
"Do Your Ears Hang Low?," 103
Dolls, 54, 145, 196, 252, 296
Dough, playing, 257z
Dress-up, playing, 186, 348
Dropping games, 26, 61
Encouragement, 85, 240
Exploration, 12, 84, 95, 345
Fairy houses, 279
Farms, 81, 98, 273, 316
Fears, 174
Feelings, respecting, 75, 161, 173
Felt, 241, 333
Filming, 200
Fingerpainting, 15, 152, 274
Fingerplays, 5, 8, 18, 77, 80, 106, 139,
    158, 199
"Five Fat Peas," 199
"Five Little Monkeys," 332
Flowers, 231, 303
"Fly Me to the Moon," 256

g, h, i

Gadgets, 118
Gardens, 50, 136, 165, 215, 319, 321
Good-bye, waving, 31
Graham cracker art, 185
"The Grand Old Duke of York," 182
Guessing game, 328
Haircuts, 20
Hammering, 79

Hammocks, 48
Hardware stores, 47
Hats, 3
"Head, Shoulders, Knees, and Toes,"
    291
Hearing, sense of, 58, 264
"Here Is a Beehive," 18
"Here We Go 'Round the Mulberry
    Bush," 283
"Hickory Dickory Dock," 56
Hiding games, 46, 72, 111, 163, 217
"How Much Is That Doggie in the
    Window?," 320
"Hush-a-Bye," 65
"I Knew a Man Whose Name Was
    Finnegan," 338
"I See the Moon," 238
"I Spy," 264, 286, 354
"I'm a Little Teapot," 177
Imitating, 1, 68, 102, 107, 120, 145,
    272, 285
"In a Cabin," 158
Independence, 24, 114, 240, 310, 326
"Intery, Mintery, Cattery Corn," 151
"It's Raining, It's Pouring," 39
"Itsy Bitsy Spider," 106

j, k, l

Jellies, 100
Jigsaw puzzles, 66, 339
Jumping, 219
Kicking, 89
Kisses, 130
Kitchen play, 6, 22, 32, 117, 121
Knee rides, 28, 63
Lanterns, 142
Laughing, 193, 276, 363
Laundry, 19, 107, 280
"Lavender's Blue, Dilly Dilly," 131
Leaves, 33, 315
Libraries, 140
"Little Ducky Duddle," 14

"The Little Train Goes up the Track," 5
"London Bridge," 267

m, n, o

Magic carpet, 206
Magnets, 308
Magnifying, 195, 335
Mail, 211
Maps, 341
Masks, 287
Massages, 59
Matching games, 55, 112, 214, 216, 244, 269, 295, 352
Mealtimes, 34, 114, 226, 236, 245, 255, 306, 343
Memory games, 101, 194, 233, 244
Messes, 71
Milk art, 175
Mirrors, 42, 88, 179
"Miss Mary Mack," 302
Mistakes, 249
Money, 340
"Monkey See, Monkey Do," 1
Movies, 330
Music, 13, 35, 86, 116, 259, 307
Musical instruments, 6, 22, 123, 128, 129, 167, 189, 212, 253, 261, 322
Name games, 157, 289, 311
"No," saying, 185
"Nobody Likes Me," 363
Number game, 354
Object permanence, 46, 111
Obstacle courses, 342
Octopus dolls, 252
"One Potato, Two Potato," 359
Oobleck, 349
Opposites, 292
Origami puppies, 334

p, q, r

Painting, 87, 104, 119, 171, 172, 197, 198, 204, 210, 221, 293, 309
Pancakes, 38
Parfaits, 305
Pattern matching, 190, 192
"Patty Cake," 164
Peekaboo, 72
Pennies, cleaning, 290
Pets, 169, 181, 188, 356
Photos, 150, 266
Picking-up games, 62, 115, 213
Picnics, 222
Pizzas, 147, 333, 343
Playgrounds, 168, 353
Potato prints, 309
Pouring game, 4
Pudding art, 172
Puppets, 144, 178, 220, 234, 325, 358
Push and pull game, 7
Questions, 345
Quiet time, 70, 86, 154
Rain sticks, 277
Rainbows, 152
Rainy days, 14, 39, 74, 83, 243
"Raspberries," blowing, 17
Restaurants, 268, 365
Rhyming, 207
"Ring Around the Rosy," 162
"Round and Round the Garden," 8
Routines, 44, 76
"Row, Row, Row Your Boat," 159

s, t, u, v

Sand play, 95, 99
Sandwiches, 232, 255, 311
Scissors, 288
Sculptures, 331
Separation anxiety, 44, 133, 161
Shadows, 234
Shapes, 190
Sharing, 208, 254, 259, 278
Shoelaces, 204
Shopping, 247, 284
"Sing a Song of Sixpence," 224
Smell, sense of, 209
Smoothies, 202
Snacks, 100, 191, 218, 229, 301, 337
Snow, 138
Social skills, 25, 31, 40, 78, 91, 92, 110, 148, 170, 180, 239
Socks, tie-dyed, 347
Sorting, 55, 112, 214, 295
Sponge art, 221
Stacking, 29, 105, 135, 137, 250
Stairs, 205
Stars, 36, 256, 350
Stickers on glass doors, 126
Strangers, 40, 92
Table, setting the, 306
"Take Me Out to the Ball Game," 346
Taste, sense of, 282, 324
Tea parties, 91
"This Is the Way the Farmer Rides," 28
"This Little Piggy," 43
"This Old Man," 2
Throwing games, 61, 69, 156
Time, 323
Tongue twisters, 313
Touch, sense of, 90, 113, 160
Toy inventory, 145
Trains, 5, 127, 258, 271
"Trot, Little Pony," 63
"Twinkle, Twinkle, Little Star," 256
"Two Little Blackbirds," 139
Undressing, 110
Visual development, 58

w, x, y, z

Walking, 67, 90, 102, 153, 243, 317
"Wash the Dishes," 77
Water play, 30, 41, 49, 88, 104, 107, 117, 248, 318
"The Wheels on the Bus," 235
"Where Is Thumbkin?", 80
Writing, 263
Xylophones, 322
Yam vines, 321
Yarn trail, 84
Yoga, 21
Zoos, 81

about gymboree

Since 1976, Gymboree has helped parents and children discover the many pleasures and benefits of play. Based on established principles of early childhood education and administered by trained teachers, Gymboree Play & Music classes emphasize the wonder of play in a noncompetitive, nurturing environment. Gymboree, which runs its interactive parent-child programs in more than 27 countries, has contributed to the international awareness of the importance of play.

consulting editors

Dr. Roni Cohen Leiderman is a developmental psychologist specializing in emotional development, positive discipline, and play. For more than 25 years, she has worked with children, families, and professionals. She is associate dean of the Mailman Segal Institute for Early Childhood Studies at Nova Southeastern University in Fort Lauderdale, Florida, and the mother of two children.

Dr. Wendy Masi is a developmental psychologist specializing in early childhood. She has designed and implemented programs for preschools, families with young children, and early childhood professionals for more than 25 years. The mother of four children, Dr. Masi is dean of the Mailman Segal Institute for Early Childhood Studies at Nova Southeastern University.

author

Nancy Wilson Hall, the mother of two children, is the award-winning author of eight books about babies, children, and families.

illustrator

Christine Coirault, a children's book illustrator based in London, is the illustrator of *How Do I Say That?* and the author of *The Little Book of Good Manners*.

photographer

Tosca Radigonda has made a career of capturing the beauty, warmth, and grace of children and families. She lives in Austin, Texas, with her husband and their son.